Fulfilling Destiny

Ceremony in the Yucatan
December 2012

Alset Publishing

ISBN: 0615916929
ISBN: 978-0615916927

FULFILLING DESTINY

Ceremony in the Yucatan December 2012

- KATHRYN V GORHAM -

Acknowledgements

When I left for the Yucatan in December 2012 I had no intention of writing a book. It was through friends asking me to connect with them during my travels and share with them upon my return that the spark was ignited. At first I jotted some notes for my own personal use and then somewhere along the way a book began to take shape.

Thank you, Henry for bringing up the idea for the trip, for encouraging me to write, and for being my way-shower. Thank you, Kathryn Hudson for planting the seed for this writing adventure while having our "back to Paris lunch" at the Village Market. Also thank you to my Third Thursday Group for your inspiration.

Thank you to the Spring Equinox ceremony group who beautifully came together to balance out the energies and the adventure and provide a superb ending to the book.

This book would not be complete without all the photographs of the adventure. My own collection was limited, because I did not take pictures with the intention of writing a book. I am extremely grateful to Carolina, Hana and Brigitte for sharing their photos with me and allowing me to use them. They have added an invaluable depth to the project. I did my best to give acknowledgement however, as the project progressed things got co-mingled and I apologize if I missed any credits where due.

A very special thank you goes out to my editors, Jan Zellers, Megan Z Crowley and Brittany Z Crowley, for their valuable work editing my rough manuscript.

CONTENTS:

Introduction:..1

Map – Yucatan December 2012 Journey....................2

Chapter 1 – The Plan 3

Chapter 2 – 2012 and Introduction 9

Chapter 3 – We Gather 15

Chapter 4 – The Adventure Begins 19

Chapter 5 – Off To Uxmal 25

Chapter 6 – Lunch and Chaya 43

Chapter 7 – Dinner and Ceremony 57

Chapter 8 – "The Day" is Here 59

Chapter 9 - Merida 91

Chapter 10 – Izamal and the Closing Ceremony.................. 105

Chapter 11- Walk to Dinner............................. 111

Chapter 12 - Dinner and Gifts.......................... 115

Chapter 13 – Lol Be The 13th Flower of Life.......................... 117

Chapter 14 – The Portal 131

Chapter 15 - Hotel Itzamaltun.......................... 134

Chapter 16 – Eh HaY U's Story 135

Chapter 17 – Lunch and Bottle Dancing.............................. 141

Chapter 18 - Chichen Itza Ceremony........................ 143

Chapter 19 – Coba and Tulum 153

Chapter 20 – Sunrise Ceremony on the Beach.................... 167

Chapter 21 - Eh Hay U 171

Chapter 22 - Spring Equinox Ceremony............................. 177

Epilogue.. 185

Introduction:

I am writing this book for those who wish to come along on my journey through the Yucatan during the December 21st, 2012 galactic alignment. This is not the only journey made at that time, far from it. There were hundreds of thousands of journeys in the Yucatan alone. This may not be the most significant or most important journey or the most amazing or even the most profound. So why write it?

It is the perspective of one individual during this alignment of galactic proportions. It is written so that you may vicariously and energetically join in the ceremonies that helped to awaken the new humanity that we are becoming.

At home in Emerald Isle, North Carolina, my like-minded friends encouraged me to bring my story home to them. They too would have liked to have made a journey for themselves during this time, but for one reason or another it didn't work out for them.

Once my friends found out I was going, they wanted to be with me energetically and share in the ceremonies. They asked me to think of them at a particular time so they could connect through me with the energies of these sacred sites during this alignment.

Those who did not go have asked and wondered, did anything happen? Has anything changed?

It is to them and to many of you who also wished to be there, that I write and share this tale. I felt compelled to go and I am so glad I did. It was a short, powerful journey that I felt like I'd been waiting for all my life. The new age is here, not just the Age of Aquarius but also so much more.

The shift is here. It's time to awaken. It's time to remember.

Map – Yucatan December 2012 Journey

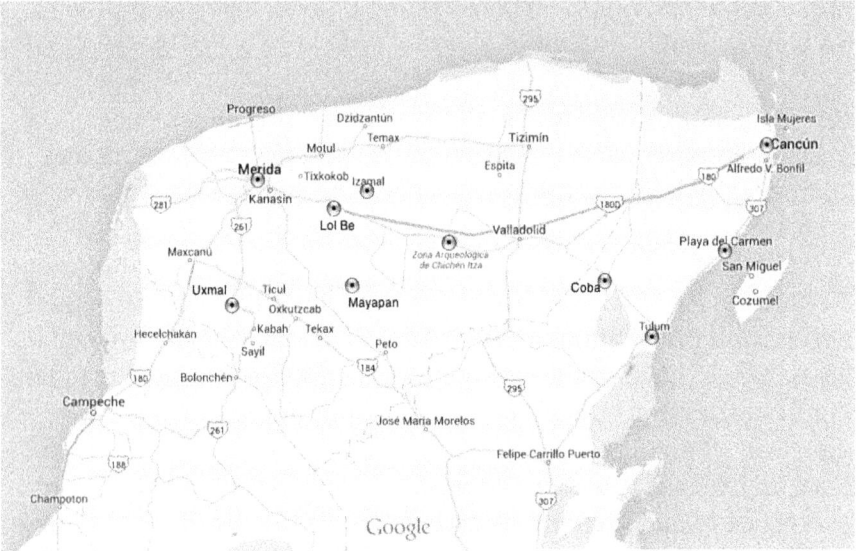

Figure 1 - Google Map Image of the Yucatan

Chapter 1 – The Plan

November 2012, Thanksgiving

Henry, my husband, is maneuvering our SUV in and out of the steadily snaking traffic along I-95 North the Tuesday before Thanksgiving. Tomorrow, the day before this national holiday, the traffic will be quite a bit heavier than what we are experiencing today. We made our travel plans to leave town a day early so that we might avoid tomorrow's rush and get a visit in at the White House while in the Washington DC area.

Maya, our black and tan mixed breed rescue puppy that we adopted this past spring, is stretched out and happily hogging the entire back seat of our SUV. I'm cozy in the passenger seat with my Wi-Fi connected and my MacBook Pro stretched across my lap. Just completing a couple of work details so I can enjoy the holiday when we reach my sister's house just outside DC.

"You know Kathryn, I've been thinking about what you said a couple of weeks ago regarding December 2012 and I think you're right. We should do something special for December 21st", says Henry.

Henry's comment is in reference to something I said a couple of weeks ago. I told him that I couldn't believe that I had booked our flights to visit family for Christmas on December 21st. For almost two decades I have been reading and studying information on December 21, 2012 and the end of the Mayan calendar. Now it was here and it just didn't feel right to let it pass as a normal day. Worse to spend the day traveling in the hustle bustle of Christmas rather than doing ceremony or in some way honoring such a milestone.

As he tells me this I am chuckling because just this morning I shared with my assistant, Brandie, I had been thinking a lot about December

21, 2012 and my desire to spend it in the Yucatan. "I want to talk to Henry about it while we're traveling for Thanksgiving."

Now riding along the highway, I marvel at how perfect it is that Spirit through Henry has introduced the idea into our conversation. In a split second, my work forgotten, I open a web browser on my computer and begin looking for 2012 tours in the Yucatan. We want to find something that is connected to the Mayans, the pyramids and ceremonies. Additionally it must be a tour that honors December 21st and December 22, 2012 as well. The 21st is the last day of the old cycle and the culmination of many cycles simultaneously. That date is the one that many worldwide are focused on. However the 22nd is the first day of the new cycle, the feminine cycle, which will last for the next 13,000 years. It too carries great importance albeit less attention in the world's focus. I bookmark a few tours websites and save them to study after the holiday.

$$\approx \approx \approx$$

Sunday afternoon, with holiday and family behind us, we are relaxing at our cottage overlooking the Pamlico River. I begin to look over the tours that I bookmarked on my computer a few days ago on our way to DC. My attention keeps getting drawn to one tour in particular. It is a tour by RMC'S Body Mind Spirit Journeys with Carolina Hehenkamp as the tour leader. It lasts through December 22nd and a few optional extension days in Playa del Carmen. It feels good to me. I call across the room to Henry and ask him to come look at it to see what he thinks.

Henry sits down on the couch beside me and takes one look at the page and says, "Carolina Hehenkamp? I was just reading about her in Drunvalo's book, *The Mayan Ouroboros*." He gets up crosses the room gets the book and returns to read me page 156:

"The next morning, a woman named Carolina Hehenkamp, who had helped us in the organization of the journey, went back to the site of the ceremony just before the Sun was rising and took some photographs of the ceremonial area. She showed me a photograph from about thirty feet away from the medicine wheel – the shells,

—

4

feathers, and rocks were all in place on the ground just as we had left them, but floating directly above the wheel a foot or so in thin air was a five pointed star that was very bright white light that the camera could easily see. Its points were rounded. Neither of us could explain how this star made it into the photograph. Carolina also took several pictures closer to the star and at different angles, but the five-pointed star was powerfully in each frame.[1]

To both of us this seems like a sign that this is the tour for us, as we had both read Drunvalo Melchizedek's books, The Ancient Secret of the Flower of Life I and II and had done the Flower of Life work shop many years ago. I had been to his Awakening the Illuminated Heart workshop in Sedona in May 2012 and we had read his other books as well, Living in the Heart, Serpent of Light Beyond 2012, and this one his newest book, Mayan Ouroboros that was released just this month, November 2012. To top it all off, earlier this month between November 8-11 we participated in Drunvalo's Awakening the Illuminated Heart workshop in Asheville NC taught by Jason Hunt and James Morrison. That settled it. The website indicates that the deadline to book a space for the trip had past. Undeterred, I decide to contact the tour company anyway and see if they would confirm space for us.

≈ ≈ ≈

After an intense couple of weeks making plans, we board a plane for Cancun on Sunday, December 16th, my birthday, to start our adventure a few days early in Playa del Carmen with some scuba diving and relaxing. We book a small boutique hotel on the beach, Fusion, and settle in for some warm weather, relaxation, dining and diving.

---

[1] Drunvalo Melchizedek, *The Mayan Ouroboros, The Cosmic Cycles Come Full Circle, The True Positive Mayan Prophecy is Revealed* (San Francisco: Red Wheel/Weiser, LLC, 2012) p. 156

Figure 2 Fusion beachfront hotel Playa del Carmen

Figure 3 Kathryn with the locals on Fifth Avenue December 16, 2012

After a few days of ocean diving and then have a special treat. A first for us, after hundreds of dives over many years, we dive in a cenote, an underground cavern. This is a very special experience with water that is crystal clear, except for the halocline.

A halocline is difficult to describe. It's a layer where the salt water and the fresh water mix to create a mysterious gelatin-like, opaque liquid where you cannot clearly focus on anything for a few minutes until you pass through it. This was unnerving, as even our dive instruments seemed masked by this foggy space and time.

Cenote diving is like diving in a cave filled with water, crystal clear fresh water. Visibility is amazing (except for the 2 or 3 minutes in the halocline). There are stalactites and stalagmites from massive to miniscule. It's like swimming through a peaceful and beautiful work of art. At one stage we popped up into an air pocket where the dive master using a flashlight pointed out tiny sea life living in these dark sunless caverns.

The caves and caverns run for miles, but for recreation diving we stay on the well marked, well known areas. Inexperienced divers can easily become lost and run out of air before finding their way out

Three and a half days of play passes quickly and now its time to meet up with our group. On the afternoon of the 20th we repack our bags and catch a cab back to the Cancun Airport Marriott to meet up with our fellow adventurers from Europe to Australia.

Figure 4 - Fifth Avenue December 2012

Chapter 2 – 2012 and Introduction

Here I'd like to present a brief introduction to 2012 itself. Many of you may be familiar with the 2012 cycle that the Mayan's call the end of time. For some, this may be a new concept. There are volumes written on the topic. I could not do justice to it by trying to reproduce all the information here, so I won't try. But I would like to give a brief overview.

In the back of the book you will find a reading list for those of you who wish to delve deeper into this information. One thing I want to say is that the information you find in the reference books is NOT the type of information Hollywood is putting out.

Just to get you in the frame of mind of this particular cycle I want to give you an analogy. When the year ends we have a celebration to honor that cycle. When ten years or a decade goes by we give a little more significance to a decade's ending. When a century passes it is a more significant milestone and there is much more focus on all that has passed and the new beginnings to come. When a millennium culminates again, the significance is heightened because you have the end of a year, a decade, a century and a millennium all at once therefore we attribute greater importance to such an event.

The 2012 cycle is very much like that. It is the culmination of many cycles at one time. The only time in our lifetime and many thousands of lifetimes that this will happen. It is the culmination of a 2,160-year cycle of the zodiac ending the Piscean Age and entering the Aquarian Age. It is the culmination of the Mayan long count cycle a 5,125-year cycle. It is the end of the 12,920-year cycle (often referenced as 13,000-year cycle, and a completion of a 26,000-year cycle (also referenced as a 25,920-year cycle). To have all of these and other cycles culminating at the same time is not the norm, but rather a rare and very powerful event. It is much more common to have them end separately rather than simultaneously.

In addition, our Earth, our moon and our sun are lining up with the center of our galaxy and will pass through this center alignment for many years. We will be in direct alignment with Hunab Ku, the Great Spirit at the center of our galaxy, at this time and not again for another 26,000 years. So the December 21, 2012 timeframe is the beginning of a time of change; a time of awakening; a time of remembering. This is not a one day phenomenon and then back to the same old normal routines and way of life. We will be in this new feminine cycle of awakening for the next 13,000 years.

When I think of 2012 the first image that comes to mind is the image from Drunvalo Melchizedek's book Flower of Life Volume I, page 56, where it shows a diagram of the precession of the equinox.

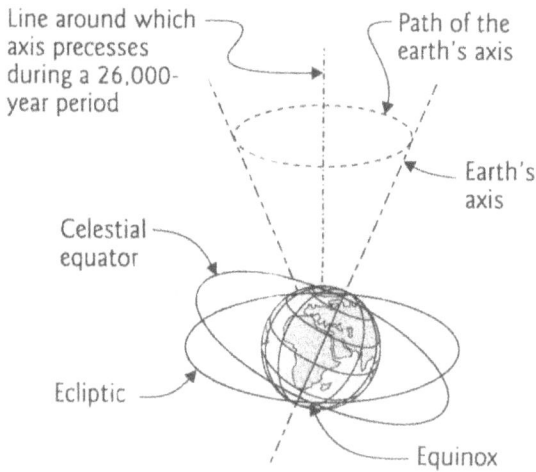

Figure 5 - Precession of the Equinoxes[2]

[2] Drunvalo Melchizedek, *The Ancient Secret of the Flower of Life Volume I* (Flagstaff, AZ: Light Technology Publishing, 1990) p. 56

Fig. 2-40. Traveling through the time period marked by the cycle of the precession of the equinoxes. The large oval is the path of the Earth's axis.
Total Revolution
= 25,920 years
Falling Asleep
D
C
1990s
A
B
Center
of
Galaxy
Awakening

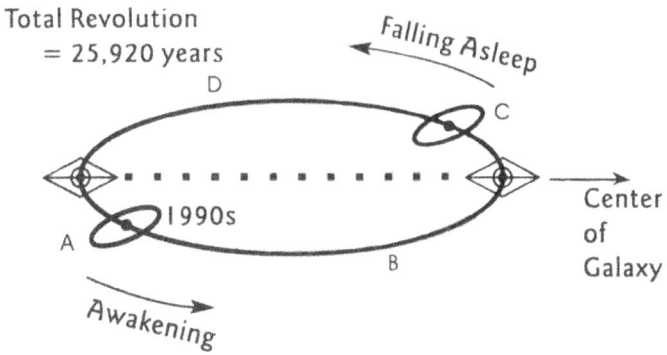

Figure 6 - Path of the Precession over 25,920 years[3]

Another image of the Precession in the book Mayan Ouroboros (Figure 7) also is very helpful to me as it ties in the signs of the zodiac as well. Showing us currently leaving the Piscean age and entering the Age of Aquarius for the next 2160 years.

---

[3] ibid.

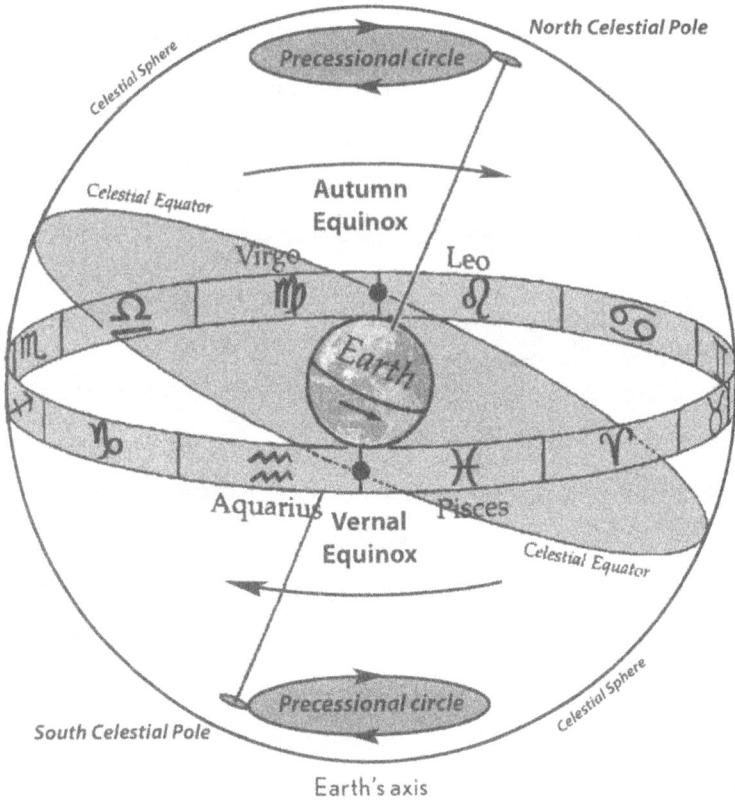

Figure 7 - Precession of the Equinoxes and the Zodiac[4]

Also a recent youtube.com video has some amazing animated graphics depicting the movements of the sun and planets. Go to YouTube.com and search for *"2012 A-Z" - A Galaxial Event of Disneyesque Proportion*. At about time marker 18 minutes he shows a hypnotic animation of our spiral rotation and travel around and forward with the sun.

---

[4] Drunvalo Melchizedek, *The Mayan Ouroboros, The Cosmic Cycles Come Full Circle, The True Positive Mayan Prophecy is Revealed* (San Francisco: Red Wheel/Weiser, LLC, 2012) p. 31

The Earth is on an axis, a tilted axis The Earth revolves around this axis giving us exposure to the sun and rotates away from the sun. This we call day and night. The Earth is also revolving around the Sun giving us what we know as our seasons and our year. The tilt of the axis also has a cycle associated with it called the Precession of the Equinoxes and is an oval shaped cycle, which takes the earth approximately 26,000 years to complete one full rotation. Inside this cycle are the 12 zodiacal cycles of 2,160 years each. The cycle is also divided into two 13,000-year cycles, one side of the cycle being male and the dark or sleeping side of the cycle and the other being female and the light or awakening side of the cycle.

At this time we are completing a male 13,000-year cycle and the Piscean age zodiacal cycle. As of December 22, 2012 we enter into the Aquarian age of the zodiac for the next 2,160 years. In addition we have begun our trip through the female side of the precession of the equinoxes that will last for the next 13,000 years from that date, December 22, 2012.

At this time, late 2012 and early 2013, it has become much easier to find the ancient knowledge coming forth that has been preserved during the male cycle (the falling asleep cycle) in order to be awakened at this time. The most common thread that is surfacing in the many varied ancient texts and knowledge pouring forth is that the heart is our most important organ and energy center in the body. It is our creation space, the place where we create from unity. It is our doorway out of polarity consciousness.

An explanation of why the heart is becoming the major focus at this time that most resonates with me is the one from Drunvalo. He tells us that long ago, 13,000 - 16,000 years ago in ancient Atlantis, we had a fall in consciousness. Prior to the fall we were at a level of consciousness where we were living from the heart in unity. After the fall we began living from the head, from the polarized brain. Since that time, many beings including the ascended masters have been helping us humans. Over thousands of years they've put ancient knowledge into place that is to be awakened now at the beginning of this new age to help us to get back to our previous level of consciousness; back to that level of unity consciousness where we're living from the heart and creating from the heart rather than from the polarized brain.

We are now in what the Mayans call a "window of time." This window spans several years. The Mayans say that changes and events to fulfill their prophecies will occur within this window of time that lasts until approximately January 2016. The key to experiencing these changes in the most peaceful and least disruptive manner is to be in our hearts. No matter what is happening, if we can be in our hearts, we will have a very unified conscious experience versus potentially going into fear and creating from polarity. From the heart we cannot create fear. When we are in fear we shall know we are in our polarized brains and not our hearts. Whatever comes in this shift, if we just live from your hearts we will be prepared.

It is believed that during and after this shift what we create will manifest much faster than today, so fast it will be almost instantaneous. Practicing now to manifest from the heart will prepare us for the coming age of instant manifestation. Without practicing now we will likely enter this new age creating from our polarized brains, creating from fear vs. love, and creating it instantly.

Gregg Braden has studied the ancient texts and indigenous prophecies of Asia and the Americas, which suggest that at this time in history something really big will happen. It's time to prepare for it now.

Chapter 3 – We Gather

December 19, 2013

The taxi driver deposits us with our luggage and dive gear in the lobby of the airport Marriott Hotel around 4:30pm. The schedule dictates that our tour bus will pick up a group of the travelers at a hotel in Cancun and then swing by the Marriott to pick up Henry, me and a couple of others. We have plenty of time so I'm taking advantage of the free wireless internet here to check in on a few work related issues before we get too far into the Yucatan and too involved with travel and ceremonies.

Five o'clock comes and goes with no sign of a bus. Henry is pacing a bit and asking me to check our travel papers to make sure we are in the correct place at the correct time. I do and we are.

While I was searching for the itinerary I notice two other ladies gathering in the same sitting area of the lobby with luggage. I speak to them and ask if they are here for the 2012 trip. Yes, they are on the same tour and they too are awaiting the arrival of the bus. The four of us introduce ourselves. It is here that Henry and I first meet Brigitte and Sophia, both from Germany. The two of them are from different cities and have just met here at the hotel lobby.

The bus eventually arrives and we roll, lift and carry our luggage out of lobby and deposit it curbside for the driver to load. This medium sized 26-seater coach becomes our second home for the next several days. I reach the top step of the bus to see a sprinkling of smiling faces and a dot here and there signifying a vacant seat. I make my way to the next to the last row of the bus before I find a pair of vacant seats for Henry and me. Brigitte and Sophia follow behind and they occupy the vacant row across the isle.

The driver apologies for being later than scheduled, but departure was slightly delayed because the flight carrying Carolina, our group leader, and the last group of travelers will be landing a bit behind schedule. We head for the airport less than a mile away and find the international arrivals terminal. The driver disappears into the terminal to check on the flight status. Returning he says the flight still has not arrived and we are free to go into the airport to get something to eat or visit the restrooms. Before we leave we are to make sure we make note of the location of the bus. Bit by bit some of the passengers venture into the airport while others remain on the air-conditioned bus.

With the delay of Carolina's flight it becomes obvious that we will not likely have dinner at the hotel when we arrive, as it will be very late. I depart the bus in search of an apple or something healthy to snack on for the three-hour ride. As I make my way around the corner I see Carolina Hehenkamp coming out of the terminal. I recognize her from the picture on the travel site. I introduce myself and point out where our bus is located. She has already connected with our driver and is waiting for the others traveling with her to exit the terminal.

As we chat it is here that I learn she has been leading a group in Peru and Bolivia since December 6, 2012. Some of that group has departed and the remainders are here to continue with us. She tells me a quick overview of where they've been: Lima, Machu Picchu, Lake of the Sun and Moon, Bolivia.

Knowing she is connected with Drunvalo and that she's been traveling in remote places and has probably had very little internet connection, I share with her Drunvalo's announcement. He is going to do a live telecast meditation at 5:11am eastern time on December 21st, 2012 where he will connect with the center of the galaxy to see if he gets a message for us.

Carolina then shares that she hadn't heard of this telecast. She goes on to say that up to about a week or so ago Drunvalo was considering joining this group for ceremony. How interesting that I keep connecting with Drunvalo in different ways and it feels like a confirmation of my teacher-training path.

The weary travelers from the December 6th group begin dribbling out of the airport and heading to the bus to deposit their luggage once again and continue their journey. It's now after 7:30pm and we roll on down the highway to Valladolid to a rest stop about half way to our destination. Here we get some quick snacks, soup or dinner and begin mingling with the other travelers. With so few men in the group Henry gravitates to Karl, a German businessman, world traveler, music lover, philanthropist and all around interesting guy who is part of the December 6th group.

After this interlude we continue rolling along the highways and Carolina, our tour leader, and ShavatY, a crystal skull keeper, introduce themselves and tell a bit about what to expect over the next few days as they lead us in ceremony. Soon our driver exits the highway and continues along the local roads with the moon shining and our headlights illuminating the trees and scrub brush. Close to midnight our bus deposits its weary group of passengers into the lobby of the Hotel Itzamaltun. As the driver quickly and efficiently unloads our luggage, Carolina connects with the desk clerk and arranges room assignments.

Minutes later Carolina calls out names and drops keys into the hands of sleepy travelers. Henry and I wheel our luggage along the path through the jungle like surroundings to find our room and rest.

Chapter 4 – The Adventure Begins

December 20, 2012 – Thursday

Figure 8 - Hotel Itzamaltún - our room to the far right (photo from hotel website www.itzamaltun.com)

I wake in Izamal this morning to the sounds of the roosters crowing and the light of the jungle filtering through the shuttered windows. My dream from last night is coming back to me.

A singer in a band has a tattoo on her chin. Actually she has multiple tattoos in circular spirals on her chin. She is playing on stage and I am in the audience sitting in the first row. She asks the audience what they thought of her new tattoo. A lady in the back row stands up and is saying it might not have been a good idea because later in life she might regret having the tattoo. The singer and I make eye contact while the woman in the back is speaking. We, the singer and I, have a heart connection and recognition. I give her my unspoken energetic consent on her tattoo. The singer makes eye contact with me several times during the performance.

I next find myself in a room with some local Realtors. The local executive officer of our county Realtor board keeps asking me where the singer is staying. I give her a street name. However that doesn't seem to satisfy her because she keeps asking me if I am sure. "Yes," I say, "that's where she's staying. Why do you ask? Did you book her somewhere else?" The executive officer responds. "Yes."

Part of what I surmise from this is that the woman in the first row and the woman in the back of the audience are both me. One woman is responding from her head and the other is responding from and connecting from her heart. The connection from the heart being a much richer and authentic experience gives me the understanding that when I'm in my heart I connect on a deep level even with our words directly with the authentic self of others. As to the Realtor connection…I am not sure what that is other than I am a practicing Realtor.

In my short meditation before breakfast I feel the energy of Mother Earth and Father Sky and then enter the tiny space of my heart. I find myself in a pyramid plaza. I do a short ceremony from inside a circle. In the north position is Metatron, in the east is Hathor, in the south is Michael and in the west is Isis and I am in the center. The energy is connected from them to me. There is a MerKaBa field surrounding us all. They are connecting with me to help me release any resistance and blocks to awakening. I feel very centered in my heart space.

After a refreshing shower and a clean set of clothes, Henry and I head to breakfast at 8:00am and find one table already filled with members of our group. We set our things at a new table and make our way to the serving counter to get some food.

≈ ≈ ≈

Figure 9 Breakfast on the veranda. Izamal, Mexico - Hotel Itzamaltun (photo by Hana)

The birds are singing in the jungle surrounding the hotel. The sun is shining as we sit in a thatched roof open veranda. Carolina and ShavatY arrive and join us at this second table. ShavatY is sharing stories of the spiritual community of locals in Playa del Carmen awakening and doing ceremony. She was concerned for a while in the early 2000s that they might not awaken, but gradually and continually more and more are called and begin awakening. I really feel her story in my heart. I am in my heart space while she is speaking. As the connection deepens tears are coming to my eyes.

ShavatY is Dutch and has been living in Playa for eleven years. She told us a bit of her story on the bus ride last night from the Cancun airport to our hotel in Izamal. Izamal is a small town in the northern Yucatan peninsula of Mexico about forty-four miles east of the city of Merida.

ShavatY tells us of working with crystals for many years and then Eh HaY U, the crystal skull, came knocking at her door (figuratively). She is to tell us more about how she came to be a crystal skull keeper during the trip. Today she is going to help us to connect to our own crystal skull energy during meditation.

I have never worked with a crystal skull or at least not in this lifetime. Given that I've been drawn to this trip, there is a strong possibility that at some point in time I may have previously worked with crystal skulls. In modern times, skulls are often portrayed as something to be fearful of. They've been associated with death in a mode of fear in the social training in the United States and maybe other areas of the world. With the Mayan end times upon us there is much talk and information coming to the forefront on crystal skulls. There is a lot of attention centered on the thirteen original Mayan crystal skulls coming back to the Mayans. Earlier this year Hunbatz Men, a Mayan elder, led a crystal skull caravan that started in New York and crossed the United States culminating in a ceremony in Los Angeles. There was even an Indiana Jones movie recently on crystal skulls that was very Hollywood, casting a layer of both intrigue and fear on the subject.

Upon doing my own investigation, what became clear to me is that crystal skulls are similar to computers. The memory in our computers is made from silicon, a living substance, due to its crystalline structure that allows it to hold an electric charge. The ancients found that quartz crystal, like silicon, is an excellent way to store information. If you lived thousands of years ago and wanted to preserve some information for the peoples of today, how would you do it?

Writing on walls would probably be obscured by time, nature and ruin. Plus, the language of thousands of years ago would most likely be undecipherable by the peoples of today. Oral tradition could have been used, but the message would likely have been transformed many, many times from the original. The meaning would most certainly not be the same as originally intended. My belief is that they tried all of the above and many other means to give, preserve and communicate their information with people of our time. I believe utilizing crystals was their best idea.

Crystals are living substances that survive for hundreds of millions of years. But why go to the time and effort to carve the crystal into the shape of a skull first before storing the information in it? Shaping the crystal into a skull designates that particular crystal as holding information for and about humans. There are many amazing and beautiful crystal clusters, points and geodes. But how would we as humans distinguish one crystal from among millions as being "the one" with information for us? We wouldn't know by site, that's for sure.

Even if we did know that a particular crystal is programmed with important information the chances are astronomical that the crystal's importance could easily be lost as it's ownership is transferred from person to another over many generations. The risk in using an unshaped crystal for such important information is a huge probability that over time it would be lost and with it the information and knowledge it was programmed to deliver. Our ancestors shaped these memory keepers into the shape of a skull to help us more easily identify their importance as keepers of knowledge.

Another reason for using a crystalline structure to preserve information for the future is that this living structure not only holds data and images, but also the thoughts and feelings of the person programming it. It is a living record of what the person recorded. One could access it would know, feel, sense and see what the recorder knew, felt, sensed and saw at the time of the recording. Now that is amazing to me. The effort it took to carve the skull had to have been herculean. It likely took years and years of skill and patience. Have you ever tried just polishing tumbled stones? Think what it must have taken to hand carve and polish a human sized crystal skull. It is my feeling that they went to such great efforts for an important reason.

Chapter 5 – Off To Uxmal

December 20, 2012

It's now after 9:30am and we are back on the bus for our ride to Uxmal, a pyramid city about two hours southwest of Izamal. Here we are to connect with our moon chakras and lunar body. Uxmal is where the Mayan priestesses studied the secrets of divine conception and tantric union, the serpent and kundalini power. After ceremony and lunch we are going to be free to explore and connect with the divine female aspect. As we would soon see, Uxmal being the center of tantric energy is portrayed through the phallic statues found there.

Figure 10 Uxmal phallic statue

Leaving the Izamal and driving through town I feel really connected to my heart energy and extremely joyful. We pass a small store with an overhead sign that reads "Tienda John" or John's Store. I feel the energy of my father with me. His name was Johnny and he owned a small mom and pop store from 1960 until his death in December of 1999.

Now I feel the energy of Granny, Maye Kathryn Wentzel Coffee, my maternal grandmother. She is here saying she is along on this trip with me now. My spiritual coach, Eddie Mullins, asked me last week if I had a family member that had crossed over perhaps, an Aunt, Mother, or someone with the name Kathryn.

"Yes," I said, "my Granny. Her middle name was Kathryn and I was named after her. "

"She is with you", Eddie said. "In fact she is so close around you that her energy is almost indiscernible from your own."

Today, I feel her with me as our small bus rolls along the road of this dry tropical peninsula. I look out over the small brush on this warm sunny December day. I am content and feeling anticipation.

≈ ≈ ≈

The city of Uxmal is teaming with buses as we arrive. Carolina gives us instructions on where the bus will be and what the plans for the day are. We disembark and stretch our legs as the driver purchases the tickets for our group inside the official archeological center. Outside the entrance the local artisans are all set up with brightly colored wares of clothing, paintings, ceramics and other craft items. Their stalls are so close to each other it is feels like one massive mall rather than the many small personal shops that they are.

With formalities completed, our group passes through the turnstiles with Carolina handing each of us a ticket as we tumble the metal arm of the gate forward. The ticket handler removes half and returns the other half of the ticket to me as he waives me into the park.

Our group forms a circle in the grass area under some trees in the shade to the left of the turnstiles before entering the pyramid city itself. Carolina explains that we are going to do a meditation. This is important to meld the energies of the two groups; the group she has been traveling with in Peru and Bolivia since December 6th, 2012 and the group that gathered in Cancun on the evening of the 19th. ShavatY has gone into the park to see if there is a more appropriate place to hold this meditation. As we await her return Carolina tells us that the Mexican government has forbidden the Mayan elders or anyone from holding ceremony at the Mayan sacred sites and especially for this time during the end times of this Mayan calendar and into the new cycle. This news comes as no surprise to me as Drunvalo Melchizedek had spoken last May of the government's position when I attended his workshop in Sedona.

She also tells us that the first pyramid we will see here today is oval, rounded on the north and south sides with stairs on the east and west sides. She tells us that this is a very, very old pyramid. It is a pyramid created by females. The age is unknown. Perhaps these female builders go as far back as Lemuria.

ShavatY returns from her scouting mission to say there is a space inside the park just east of the oval pyramid where there is shade and a good place for our meditation.

Figure 11 Uxmal - The Oval Pyramid 12-20-2012 – Our group entering

Our group moves forward up the stairs and into the pyramid city of Uxmal. At the top of the stairs we are right in front of the main temple. I stop just to admire this beautiful structure. I breathe in the energy and connect to this awesome structure. My hands light up with energy. They are tingling and vibrating and they stay active throughout the visit. (Actually just writing about this at home now my hands are tingling as I bring up that memory.) I snap a photo as I am really enjoying the energy and the view of this beautiful oval, feminine pyramid, known today as the Pyramid of the Magician.

Slowly the group takes in the views while entering the park. One by one we join ShavatY under the trees on the east side of the oval pyramid. Each joins the circle on the ground around the altar being set up for the group integration meditation. She has placed Eh HaY U, the crystal skull, on the altar, some corn, and other sacred objects and invites group members to place any crystals or objects on the altar that they have brought to the ceremony. I place my crystal point and clear crystal quartz stones that I brought from home to gather this energy. Upon my return home I will gift these stones to my "Third Thursday Group" members.

Figure 12 - Altar December 20, 2012 Uxmal (photo by Hana)

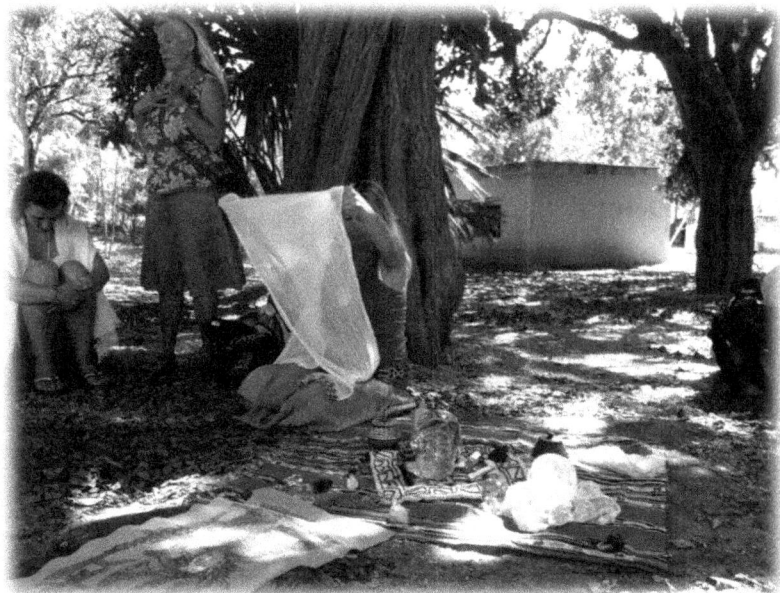

Figure 13 Uxmal - Merging the Two Groups Meditation 12-20-2012 (photo by Hana)

ShavatY is explaining that she did not travel with the first group for the full term of their trip in Peru and Bolivia, however she and Eh HaY U did gather with them for ceremony for two days. At the end of the second day's ceremonies she was standing there with her arms wrapped around her pink backpack transporting Eh HaY U when one of the elders from the ceremony walks up to her and standing face to face he asks her why she is here?

"I don't know. I just felt I had to be here," she replies.

With that said the elder disappears into a nearby hut and comes back with a large sack. Inside the sack are many ears of maize or corn. He explains that they are gifts to him from other elders and shamans from all over South America who have visited him and his village. He has been collecting and saving these for many, many years.

He looks at ShavatY and holds the bag out to her and says, "Choose one."

Figure 14 Alter set for the 12-20-2012 meditation

She is so overwhelmed with emotion that she cannot respond and instead of saying anything she just starts crying with tears streaming down her face and her arms folded around Eh HaY U. The elder on seeing this reaction reaches into the sack selects an ear of corn and pulls it to himself to retain and then hands the remainder of the corn and the sack to ShavatY as a gift.

What the elder did not know and what had caused the depth of the response from ShavatY is that one of the guides or goddesses that she works with is the Lady of the Corn. This connection with the Lady of the Corn makes the generous gesture from the elder deeply moving and very personal to ShavatY.

30

She shows us an ear. To me it looks like a miniature ear of what I would call Indian corn; the kind that we used when I was a child to decorate for fall. The ears ShavatY has are about four to five inches long, about an inch to and inch and a half in diameter and still have the dried husks covering the kernels. The kernels themselves are a deep, dark red-brown color.

The circle is being completed as the last of our group arrives to fill in around the altar. Others are adding their stones and sacred items to the altar as ShavatY is in the middle of the story of the corn. Suddenly a uniformed male park guard wearing a white shirt with official emblem and a khaki green hat, with a female companion in light blue and two park workers, one male and one female, wearing orange shirts and black pants, strut hurriedly towards us. In Spanish the male guard interrupts our group sternly conveying that we cannot do ceremony. ShavatY and Carolina speak up saying we are not doing ceremony, but rather a meditation only.

The guard retorts that we cannot bring tools or foreign objects into the park. These things are not in harmony with the energy of the pyramid and we are prohibited from using them.

Our group looks in astonishment at this simple man in uniform, and then among ourselves perplexed as to his commands. Carolina and ShavatY both readily consent to the wishes of the order following guards directive to put away all crystals and altar items, i.e. "tools." It is understood that we may do the meditation, but without "tools."

Ok, time for plan B. As we are packing up the altar items ShavatY tells us dimensionally all the articles on the altar are still there in the other dimensions and will be there for our meditation dimensionally. In case of such an incident ShavatY has prepared an altar in a cloth bag that will serve as the energetic altar rather than a visual altar. We continue putting away our crystals, Eh HaY U, the corn and all the other items.

We move a few feet to the north where there is a short, square wall made of stone about six feet across. The Peru group sits on the wall facing out representing the inner circle. The new group of travelers sits on the ground facing them. The Peru group is instructed to open their hearts and allow the love to radiate. The new group is to feel this radiating love and then open their hearts and reciprocate. No guidance is given during the actual meditation.

I go into my heart space and can feel the energy grow. The prana in my heart is glowing and growing with each in breath and each out breath. At some point in the meditation I sense ShavatY walking around. She visits those in the inner circle and then comes to each of the new arrivals in the outer circle. When she gets to me she touches my hand to indicate that I am to open it. When I do she drops in a kernel of the ancient energy corn that had been gifted to her recently in Peru. At that moment my eyes are closed and I don't know what has been placed into my hand. All I know is that she put "something" into my hand.

At the moment when she places the kernel into my palm my third eye inner light becomes pink. Pink is not a regular color for me in my third eye vision; in fact I can't remember seeing that color before this time. Then I feel the love from the outer circle like a wave flowing back and forth between us. This continues a while then I see in my inner vision two bubbles one on top of each other like the figure eight and then they merge and become one like a circle or sphere.

Next ShavatY is guiding the Peru group one by one from their sitting position on the wall and walking them to a space in the outer circle and seating them on the ground between and among the members of the new group. We literally become one group. Someone sits next to me, later I come to know it was Sue from Australia.

As the meditation continues Sue reaches over to tap me, to let me know the circle is joining hands to connect as one group in one circle. I am a bit startled as I was deep in meditation. I reach to my left to let the next person know and I take the hand of Erik, a teenager from Germany. As I take his hand I drop my kernel of corn. I start to think and fret about finding the dropped kernel and then let it go from my mind knowing I can look after meditation.

32

The meditation completed we cross our hands over our hearts. ShavatY instructs us to next walk in silence as a group to the west side of the oval pyramid. Before leaving Henry, Sue and I are digging around in the dirt looking for my kernel.

Carolina comes by and says, "It's perfect. It's returned to Mother Earth."

≈ ≈ ≈

With that we depart for the west side of the oval pyramid, The Pyramid of Magic, in a walking meditative state. I am popping in and out of my heart and meditative state thinking about that little kernel. My ego wants to possess it. It was amazing energy when it came to me. My head is saying it wants to keep the kernel to reconnect with that energy. Another part of me is still dropping into the heart and feeling the energies around me and knowing that it is perfect, as Carolina has said. I arrive at the courtyard still vacillating back and forth. I'm even contemplating asking ShavatY for another kernel. Each time the need to possess comes up I reconnect with the heart energy of knowing it is perfect.

Figure 16 The West side of the oval pyramid

Figure 17 Close up of the upper portal entrance - Oval pyramid

Gathered in the courtyard on the west side of the pyramid ShavatY begins again with the story of the corn from where the guards interrupted her earlier. She then instructs us to wander the grounds feeling the energy of the pyramids and Mother Earth. While wandering each person in the group is to feel the connection with these energies and be drawn to a spot to place their kernel somewhere on the grounds.

This act of returning the kernel to Mother Earth will combine the sacred energy of Peru and all the ancient sites of South America that the corn came from with the energy here in Mexico. We are NOT permitted to save the kernel and take it with us. It must be returned to Mother Earth in order to bring in the ancient energies and to integrate them with the sacred and ancient energies on the site we are visiting. As ShavatY is speaking I see in my inner vision an energetic grid on the earth forming from the sacred energies represented in the corn that has been gifted over many years from many places and the connecting energy to the places that the kernels are now being placed.

When I heard the final instructions from ShavatY, that we are in no way permitted to keep the kernel and our mission is to find an energetic connection to gift it back to mother, I laugh inside. I have certainly completed that part. What better spot could I possibly have found to share my kernel than the spot where the two bubbles merged into one in my meditation, the spot where the love was flowing in waves, the spot where the kernel itself chose to leave my hand and not be found.

≈ ≈ ≈

We walk around in contemplation and connection for a half hour and then are to meet at the restaurant near the park entrance for lunch. I am on my way to the restaurant and I pause once again at the top of the steps to look back at the magnificent magic oval pyramid. I am admiring her and taking a couple of pictures using my special effects app on my phone when Carolina passes by on her way to lunch. I asked about this oval shape and if there are other pyramids with this shape. Carolina tells me this is the only known oval pyramid on earth.

She sees me admiring the beautiful structure and says to me, "Maybe we built this."

"Yes," I reply with a glow inside, "maybe we did."

Carolina had read my thoughts. During my time of wandering and connecting I sensed that I (and possibly others in this group) had been here many lifetimes ago when this amazing oval structure was built. Smiling inside and out, I turn and exit the park to meet up with the group for lunch.

Figure 18 Oval Pyramid shot with FXCamera app when leaving for lunch (mirror image)

Figure 19 - Uxmal symbols on ruins

Figure 20 Uxmal - symbol reminded me of the Fibonacci sequence

Figure 21 Uxmal 12-20-2012

Figure 22 Uxmal symbols 12-20-2012

Figure 23 Plaza west of the oval pyramid - connecting with the energy

Figure 24 Intricate bird carvings

Figure 25 Amazing arched roof

Figure 26 Oval pyramid stairs on the West side

Figure 27 Uxmal oval Pyramid of the Magician (photo by Hana)

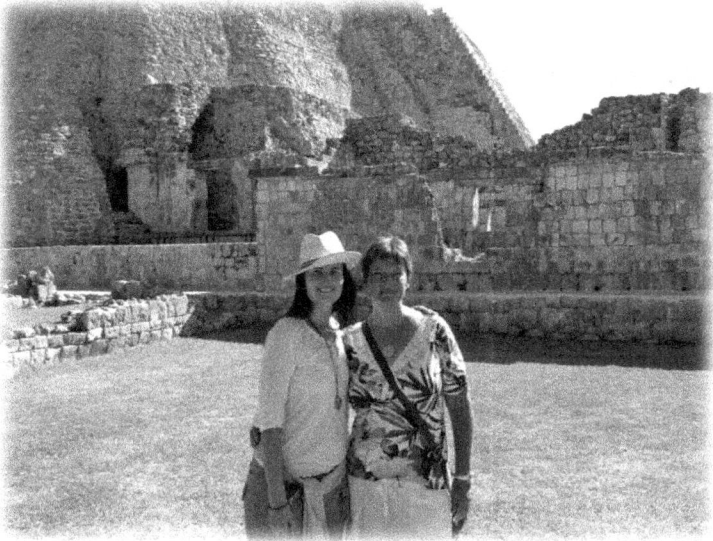

Figure 28 - Hana & Helga (photo by Hana)

Chapter 6 – Lunch and Chaya

December 20, 2012

Our group occupies three long tables in the restaurant inside the park. ShavatY sits at our table and introduces us to chaya, a green drink made from Mayan spinach. This restaurant's version of chaya is mixed with orange juice and pineapple juice. In other places you will find different mixtures. It feels like and instant boost of energy and the taste is quite good as well. One of the tablemates orders a soup with chaya in it. I order chaya that I eat on a tortilla with guacamole. Henry, contrary to his normal appetite and adventurous eating habits, eats some, but very little. He does enjoy the chaya drink, as does the whole table. We drink three of four pitchers.

ShavatY asks Sue, our barefoot friend from down under, to watch the backpack with Eh HaY U in it while she visits the ladies room. Sue asks me to take over when she left the table for a minute. I feel honored to be watching over this intriguing crystal skull for a few minutes until ShavatY and Sue return.

≈ ≈ ≈

After lunch we reenter the park turnstiles with our tickets and the plan is to do a ceremony. Our group coalesces on the south side of the now familiar oval pyramid where Carolina explains that with the guards watching us so closely we would not do a formal ceremony. Instead we will walk the grounds feeling the dimensional portals as we reverently and silently walk in a loosely meandering group.

Figure 29 Group gathers after lunch [photo by Hana]

At a pile of rock ruins there are iguanas sunning themselves and Carolina and ShavatY take a moment to share with us their purpose. These ancient creatures are the guardians and energy keepers of the pyramid sacred sites. The iguanas hold and have been holding for many centuries the ancient energies in these sites that have been lost to modern awareness until very recently when the sites have been re-discovered and to a small degree restored.

Figure 30 Iguana guardians of the ancient energies [photo by Brigitte]

On we walk, connecting to the energy of the place. I come to an open area with the ball court on my right. Past the ball court is a doorway that leads back to the area of the oval temple that is looming over the whole plaza. As I look up I am overwhelmed with emotion. The words, "I'm back," pass through my brain. I drop into my heart and feel grief and connection. It is such a familiar site, yet in this lifetime I have never seen it before this moment. I feel as if I have looked thousands of times through the ball court and through this doorway that leads to a complex now labeled "The Nunnery" on the tourist maps. It is so familiar.

Figure 31 Ball court at Uxmal with Portal at the north end

Figure 32 Close up of the portal at the north end of Ball court

I am very grateful that we are walking in contemplation rather than in conversation. Had I been in conversation I might have missed this connection and this gift of recognition would have been lost, maybe forever. Wow, it takes my breath away. I just breathe it in and feel the joy of reconnection.

As we continue our "group" becomes smaller, scattered groups rather than one large group. Before long we find ourselves in front of the steps of the Great Pyramid, which the public is permitted to climb. One by one a few members of our group make the ascent, though some choose not to. Others are still scattered about.

I am wandering the ruins in front of the Great Pyramid not yet ready to go up. I notice that the pink backpack that ShavatY carries is sitting on the ground with no one around it. I instantly feel protective of Eh HaY U and stop to look around for ShavatY. Sure enough she is not far away, but her back is to the pink sack and I don't feel comfortable just walking away. I stay near by and look at symbols on the ruins. I am in the shade here and it feels quite good. The temperature here in the tropics in December is quite warm bordering on hot, especially in the sun. Water is a must to stay hydrated.

My concerns about Eh HaY U ease. I see he is safe, his backpack facing the stairs of the Great Pyramid with others from our group sitting or walking near by including ShavatY. I venture towards the steps for my climb to the top.

As I begin climbing, Carolina is also making her way up. She is explaining to those in our group within earshot that one should treat each step as an initiation. Stop when the energy changes at the major platforms to feel it and to integrate it. I slowly and contemplatively climb the steep steps in an angular ascent.

Figure 33 North face of the Great Pyramid Uxmal

Figure 34 Carolina on the steps of the Great Pyramid Uxmal 12-20-2012

When I reached the top I look closely at the symbols as I have been seeing all day. I notice that, like other places in Uxmal, I am seeing intertwining pairs of lines that remind me of DNA. The thought occurred to me that being here could be activating our DNA in some way. It could be one of the purposes of this place and the other pyramid sites.

Figure 35 - Uxmal 12-20-12 symbols atop the Great Pyramid

Figure 36 - Uxmal 12-20-12 symbols atop the Great Pyramid

Figure 37 - Uxmal 12-20-12 Symbols atop the Great Pyramid

I also notice from this top view that Henry is near the bottom sitting down on the lower steps. I'm not sure why he hasn't ascended. I know it is his choice and honor that he is doing what he wants, but it feels odd. I wonder if there is something going on for him.

Figure 38 Looking down from the top of the Great Pyramid. ShavatY and Eh HaY U watching us

I take a few pictures from this breathtaking vista. To the north is this strange ornate tall wall. It is the only way I can describe it. On the tourist maps it is labeled the "house of doves."

Figure 39 - View to the north from the Great Pyramid

Figure 40 - Ornate wall labeled the House of Doves

From this vantage point I am looking at the wall from its thin side edge. There seems to be a face in the end of the wall facing me. This structure on the archeological maps of the site is referred to as the House of the Doves.

Figure 41 Face in the wall ... see circle

After shooting a few snapshots I sit to meditate. While in meditation I kept getting a bit of fear coming up over the descent. I also sense I may be picking up the fear of others. I know that is a lesson for me, a test. Feel the fear and whatever else comes up and still move forward. So with that, I begin my decent.

The feelings come and go. I continue my initiation steps slowly, one at a time. The fear changes to joy then I connect with Eh HaY U. His pink backpack is on the ground facing the steps with ShavatY and a handful of others from our group sitting a few feet away on a bench. As I step down each step I say his name. It becomes a different journey down the steps. He becomes a connection, a helper along the way.

As I am descending, I notice Henry is no longer sitting on the steps of the pyramid. When I reach the bottom of the Great Pyramid I find him off to the left sitting in the shade. We make our way to the west where the beautiful ornate wall is standing. This same wall I saw from the top that had the face in the end facing me, the one that is called the House of the Doves.

Figure 42 - House of Doves showing the portal

≈ ≈ ≈

The wall is in my estimation about seventy-five to one hundred feet long. In the middle of the base there is a portal or doorway, and above that there are peaks with holes in them of intentional ornate design the entire length of the wall. With my back to the wall and facing away across an expanse of lawn and into the jungle I see there was once a stair case leading down that no longer exists except for some remnants of ruins. Scattered in the grassy area and jungle are large chunks of round columns, broken and lying about.

The thought that comes to me is that the female energy in sacred geometry is round and curved. The male energy is angular, square and straight lines. This may be the only oval or rounded pyramid in all of Mexico or all of Mayaland, which means it could be the only female energy temple site in all of Mayaland. What a perfect place to bring in the energies of this new feminine age that is birthing itself in less than two days on December 22, 2012.

The energy of this place is still buzzing me. I walk back to the great pyramid and sit on the steps of the north face. Eh HaY U's backpack is still on the ground, now directly in front of me. I begin meditating and connecting to his energy. I am feeling my third eye pulse and my lips pulse.

Then Henry comes and sits beside me, saying he doesn't feel well. He pours some of the drinking water over his head. I know that something is off, because under normal circumstances he wouldn't waste the drinking. He then tells me he feels dehydrated. I insist he finish that bottle of water. I walk over to ShavatY and the group with her and let them know we are heading back to the entrance for water. Carolina and the last of our group are now descending the Great Pyramid.

It is about a half of a mile back to the entrance. Just as we are about a hundred yards from the exit Henry says, "I'm feeling sick. I think I have to throw up."

Luckily we are just a few feet past a rest room, the only rest room inside the park. We retreat a few steps and he enters the men's room. Sure enough, he throws up three times in succession moments after entering. He says he feels a bit better after that and we continue on to the turnstiles. Henry veers off to the left toward the restaurant to buy some water and me off to the right to explore the shops to find any medications to help his unsettled stomach. Instead I find a first aid station.

I communicate to the attendants in the first aid station in a combination of Spanish and English that my husband is ill and I am looking for some medication. They direct me to a van with a doctora just outside in the parking lot. Doctora Sandy, a young and kind Mexican doctor, checks Henry over. We both, Doctora Sandy and I, speak in English-Spanish combinations with vocabulary limitations, but communicate well enough to reach understanding. She gives him four packs of electrolytes to combine with water to replenish him over the next couple of days. She gives him some pills to help protect his stomach. After being supplied with meds and having vomited he is feeling a little better.

≈ ≈ ≈

54

We congregate at the park entrance and the group gathers near the bus for the two-hour ride back to Izamal. Carolina lets us all know that we would do the ceremony that we didn't get to do at Uxmal tonight at the hotel upon our return. Our group is no different than the Mayan elders who are being resigned to doing ceremony on their own private grounds rather than at sacred sites. The fear of the government is so apparent. The people themselves, the park workers, are curious, even excited and accepting about the ceremonies, but it is not worth losing their job over.

Upon arrival in Izamal a few folks want to skip dinner and return to the hotel. Henry is in that group. The bus driver stops at the restaurant and unloads all those going to dinner and then takes the remainder back to the hotel. Henry wants to join the ceremony that we will have after dinner so he heads home to rest up. Food is not something appealing to him right now.

Chapter 7 – Dinner and Ceremony

December 20, 2012

The restaurant Kinich El Sabot de Izamal welcomes our group with open arms and one very long table. No one orders individual meals instead the staff just brings samples of dishes such as empanadas, salads, and curious but tasty things to which I can't put a name. We all happily share family-style. Once again today, we drink pitchers of Chaya, the Mayan spinach drink. Near the end of dinner Carolina announces that the bus will leave at 3:00am for our December 21st ceremony at Mayapan. It is a change to the original plan. The change is set into motion so we can be doing ceremony at 5:11am local time (11:11am universal time). Wow, 3:00am? That means that Henry better be feeling well in order to join us.

The bus deposits us back to the hotel at 8:30pm. A quick stop in our rooms and then we gather in the grass area off the pavilion and spa for the ceremony we couldn't do at Uxmal.

≈ ≈ ≈

Henry has been resting while we enjoyed dinner and feels well enough to participate in the meditation. Our group sits in a circle on the grass with the night stars shining overhead. ShavatY tells us about Eh HaY U and how he and she work with energy on many dimensions. I wish I could remember all that she is saying. It is amazing and fascinating.

This is our connection with Eh HaY U. He has "peaked" at us energetically while we were climbing the pyramids today at Uxmal, but this is our first connection as a group. ShavatY speaks multi-dimensionally and conveys esoteric knowledge in a package that is easy to understand. In the meditation, we will connect with the crystal skull consciousness of Mother Earth and crystal skull consciousness grid. There are millions of grids around the Earth. Every life form must have its own grid.

Eh HaY U's consciousness helps us to find our own personal crystal skull consciousness to connect with. ShavatY tells us that during the meditation we might see a crystal skull in our inner vision in front of us coming toward our face or glowing in front or even merging with our own skull. The meditation begins. We connect inside with the Earth's grid for the crystal skull consciousness. During meditation ShavatY walks around outside the circle and places Eh HaY U on the top of each of our heads from behind.

The skull feels heavy and is facing the out in the same direction as our own skull and face. Inside in my meditation I see the skull and he comes to me and merges with my heart. I am in the sanctity of my tiny space of the heart and the skull is glowing and then becomes red in color and then blue. ShavatY finishes by telling us that this is to help us prepare for the ceremony on December 21, 2012, tomorrow, the unification of the Condor and the Eagle.

Chapter 8 – "The Day" is Here

December 21, 2012

When I'm finally sleeping soundly after several hours of fitful sleep, a gentle knock sounds at my door. It is 2:30am. So much has happened with travel, integration and Henry not feeling well that caused me to go to bed anxious. Henry also hears the knock and alerts me. I stretch awake to find he's been up several times during the night with diarrhea. He knows he can't do a two-hour bus ride and then an hour or more of ceremony without a bathroom near. I unpack his belongings from my day bag and head off with the group.

The ride is quiet as most of us are still half dozing. In the pitch-black morning about 4:20am the bus rolls onto the grounds of Mayapan pyramid park. The sky is dark and clear, a blessing since at midnight it had rained heavily and had drizzled during our drive.

≈ ≈ ≈

On the bus with the windows darkened from the blackness of the night, ShavatY speaks with us about why we are here at this location for this special day. She tells us about a vision she had years ago about a Condor that was shot and fell from the sky. A little girl found it and began healing it. Once the Condor was healed and well, he stayed close to the little girl through womanhood and a great love grew between them. After this vision she was instructed to find the place of the Condor and the Eagle and, once found, she was to reunify them. The search began.

Eventually she found the Condor and the Eagle. The place where she found them was Mayapan. She had come to Mayapan to do ceremony. Often people who do ceremony join other ceremonial groups that are there. It is assumed that for some reason you are guided to join them and that all is in divine order. ShavatY saw a group there doing ceremony and joined. While sitting in meditation she got the feeling she was being guided to go somewhere. Upon opening her eyes to look around her attention was drawn to a bright blue flower petal on the ground, just one petal. She felt guided and compelled to follow it. So she got up and moved in that direction. Soon she came to a place where there were two more blue flower petals separated by some distance. She knew there was something about them. She sensed that they marked a spot. She had a knowing that she was to sit on the ground in between the two petals. She moved to the spot between them and sat down. Whoosh, she immediately got a rush of energy. These two blue flower petals were marking a portal of vortex energy.

ShavatY just sat between the petals and received a download of energy. When the download completed she opened her eyes and that was when she "found" it. She had found the Condor and the Eagle. There they were just a few feet away on the wall of the pyramid staring back at her. At this moment ShavatY felt she had completed her task, but it was not true. This was 2003 and she had completed the "finding" of the Eagle and the Condor, but she could not reunite them. It was not time.

On the wall of the pyramid there is an excavated section of an inner pyramid. Many pyramids are built over previous pyramids. On this exposed wall of the inner pyramid she found a three dimensional relief of a Condor on the left and the Eagle on the right with a human body between them. She tells us there is something about it that she wants us to see for ourselves. When we go inside we will understand. She says she could tell us about it, but she feels it's important that we see it for ourselves.

She continues talking about Quetzalcoatl or Kukulkan the feathered serpent. Around his neck he wore a necklace made of very colorful bird feathers He came from the stars and crossed Mexico and came to Chichen Itza. He taught the people and passed along his wisdom for many years here. Wars came and he could no longer remain there. So he and a few disciples moved north and created Mayapan. Here he continued to teach and share his wisdom. This is the time, December 21, 2012, that he planned for the reunification of the Condor and the Eagle.

The Condor from the South represents Mother Earth and all the pain and suffering she has endured at the hands of humans. The Eagle from the north represents man, humans, and all the pain and suffering man has inflicted on man. Our mission today is to reunite these two energies the South and the North.

≈ ≈ ≈

The park is not open yet, as it is only 4:40am. It will officially open at 8:00am, but given the importance of this day it's possible that it may open a little earlier. Before we go inside we will do a meditation and ceremony outside the gate and walls in an area facing the main pyramid, in alignment with the energy of the pyramid.

We exit the bus under the guidance of a couple of flashlights and set up the altar on the ground outside the walls of Mayapan. ShavatY lays out the altar cloth; onto it she places the white corn representing the energy of the new age that is dawning this day. There is one vessel in each of the four corners representing the four directions East, South, West, and North. The gifted red corn representing the ancient knowledge that is re-awakening in these times goes onto the altar. Eh HaY U is the center and the anchor. Crystals and other items from the group members are placed around as well to complete the altar. ShavatY choose this area because we are in direct alignment with the pyramid. We form a circle and connect with our hearts to Mother Earth's crystal skull consciousness and our own crystal skull consciousness to begin the ceremony with a meditation.

Figure 43 - Altar December 21, 2012 (photo by Carolina)

I also call in the energy of my friends who have asked me to connect with them on this special day from this mystical location. To my friend and angel worker, Kathryn Hudson, of Emerald Isle and Paris, France I invite you to join this group and me as we begin our ceremony. Ahna Logan, my artist friend from Pine Knoll Shores, NC I invite you and your spirit to join us as we honor this time and this day. Henry, my beloved, just a few miles away and so much wanting to be here in person I connect with you so that you too are here as a part of our group. Last, I call my fellow seekers, who make up the Third Thursday Group in Emerald Isle, come be with us as we make the shift of ages, as we align with awakening energy at the center of the galaxy for the first time in 26,000 years.

≈ ≈ ≈

After this connection and upon ShavatY's signal our group stands and forms two lines: a north line representing the Eagle and a south line representing the Condor. The two lines stand facing each other. Each person opens his or her heart. The southern representatives offer their wounded Condor to the person facing opposite them in the north line. The northern representatives in return offer their wounded Eagle to their partner in the south to be healed. After a few minutes of this energy exchange the partners north and south embrace each other. This is the healing and cleansing ceremony before the reunification can take place.

During this healing and cleansing of the energies of the Eagle and the Condor I am in the south line representing Mother Earth. I am receiving the wounded Eagle energy, the energy of the man's cruelty to man. I think of my heritage. The ancestors on my father's side are Spanish and I receive images of the conquistadors in the Americas. I see in my inner vision how both human bodies and sprits were harmed. What took place was the killing and the destruction of their physical beings and their spiritual heritage.

My maternal grandmother was born in the USA in 1907 and her family name was Wentzel from Germany. I feel the pain that man has dealt to man in that country. I am hugging Bettina who lives in Germany. She is too young to have been alive during World War II, even so I feel that her wounded Eagle is coming to heal some of the pain that country has borne over the years. Then images of other cruelties man has inflicted on man and Mother Earth come to my heart. I am grieving. I am open.

The images come to me like clips in a newsreel being played at a fast speed. I see images of war, murders, unkindness, children being slapped, verbal abuse, stealing, deceit, and images of Mother Earth being blasted for mining, oil spills, industrial pollution, cars, land and trees being bulldozed, bombs falling, explosions underwater, HAARP, litter and garbage, rivers polluted and on these images play. These images of how disconnected we are from Mother Earth and each other flash and the emotions are felt deeply.

My partner, Bettina, (the mother of our teenager Erik) speaks only German, which I do not speak. However at this moment spoken language is irrelevant. It is a very, very emotional embrace. We are both crying and connected at our hearts and healing the wounds to Mother Earth and humanity. I'm not sure we could have broken the embrace, if we had wanted to, here on this dark star lit morning thousands of miles from our homelands. The connection with the group energy creeps into my consciousness and I sense everyone on both sides of the lines embracing and crying and healing.

I had not sensed or imagined how emotional and powerful this ceremony and connection would be. Even as I type this I feel its power again flood over me and it's difficult to describe its depth. It is extremely emotional and moving.

Figure 44 - Outside Mayapan, December 21, 2012 (photo by Hana)

≈ ≈ ≈

After the partners north and south connect for a several minutes, each in their own time returns to the circle to continue the meditation under the still dark sky. Many, including me, are still crying from the emotional connection that came from healing the wounded Condor and Eagle. As the emotions settle and we return to our meditative state ShavatY again comes around with Eh HaY U and connects the crystal skull with each of us.

While awaiting ShavatY's visit Mindy, our New York City girl, enters into her meditation. As the meditation progresses she has a strong feeling she is being guided to open her eyes and look. She is not sure why, but she does it anyway. Upon following her guidance and opening her eyes she is greeted with the site of a shooting star. This is extra special for her, an answer to her asking. Since she lives in the city with all the light pollution, she rarely sees the stars. It is a big desire for her on this trip to see the stars. As an added exclamation point she is also gifted with the site of a shooting star on this special morning.

Soon I sense ShavatY as she approaches me from the front. First she places Eh HaY U so that he and I are touching nose to nose. After that she adjusts him so that we are linking forehead to forehead. Next she moves the skull away from the forehead and places Eh HaY U against my heart.

Wow. When she moves Eh HaY U away from my forehead to my heart I instantly get a strong feeling of peacefulness and hear in my inner voice, "ahhh." Then a knowingness comes over me that I'm leaving my head and going to live in the heart. It is a profound revelation and sensation. It's hard to put into words. It is a feeling of connecting to a greater part of me and humanity all at once.

It felt like energetic taffy, as if Eh HaY U was drawing everything out of my head with a pulling sensation leaving behind just empty space. Then she placed that energy that was drawn out of my head into my heart when the crystal touched my body. The process brought both powerful feelings and images.

ShavatY continues on around the circle connecting the crystal skull with the others. The meditation continues until the gray light breaks in the sky. I see a couple of stars and a satellite blinking its way from north to east as I open my eyes at the end of the meditation.

≈ ≈ ≈

After the ceremony the morning light brightens in the sky and we are still the only ones in the park (well not "in" the park but outside the park walls). For the first time we can see our surroundings. We are in the dirt parking area outside the pyramid park surrounded by short stonewalls topped with barbed wire. ShavatY, kneeling next to the altar cloth once again gifts us one single kernel of the ancient energy corn to use later today inside Mayapan.

She also tells us that the white corn in the four corners represents the four directions. She invites us to help ourselves to these kernels. We are to take as much as we want if we so choose. Taking the white corn means we agree to take it back to our homes and use it in ceremony. We are to bring this new energy that has just been birthed to other parts of the world and spread it and share it through ceremony, especially from now through March 21, 2013, the spring equinox. At the equinox the energies being birthed here today, on the shortest, darkest day of the year, will balance out and take hold. Her only request is that we leave at least one kernel in each bowl so she has enough for the next ceremony.

I help myself to some of this white corn to take with me and I retrieve my personal items from the altar, as that is being disassembled. From here we head off on our own in different directions to connect with the energy of the area, of Mother Nature, to be with our inner guidance and to integrate this powerful energy and experience.

As I walk, there is a bird that catches my eye. He/she is gorgeous. The bird is teal colored for the most part with an amazing and unusual tail. The tail is about four to six inches long and very thin until the very end where it fanned out. [I look up the birds of the Yucatan later and I believe this to be a Turquoise-browed Motmot.]

—

Figure 45 - Mayapan 12-21-12 Motmot (see circle)

I point out this beauty to others and soon many in the group are noticing and hearing birds.

About 7:00am the first workers start showing up and another car of people arrives and they start doing yoga and stretching. Carolina makes her way over to talk with the guard. She works her magic and gets permission for us to enter the park before it officially opens. And another note of particular importance is that at this point we also get access to the park's bathroom!

Now that we have permission Carolina wants us to enter the park together as a group. A few at a time walk the pathway to the entrance and stop here to wait for the wandering group to collect at the entrance of this ancient pyramid city. As we wait everyone is absorbing the sites and sounds around us when someone catches a glimpse of a beautiful red bird in the trees to our right. Next the teal bird shows up again. It could be the same bird or a friend. Then a hummingbird flies right past us and hovers around a nearby palm tree allowing our group to admire its beauty. A little later a beautiful yellow bird joins into the energy.

When I recount these sightings to ShavatY later, she connects the colorful bird sightings with Kukulkan/Quetzalcoatl, the feathered serpent, who created Mayapan and to the fact that he wore a necklace of many colorful feathers called his rainbow necklace. It is as if the birds are thanking us for performing the ceremony of uniting the Eagle and the Condor. It is as if the energy of Kukulkan/Quetzalcoatl himself is with us.

Figure 46 - ShavatY and Eh HaY U waiting for the group at the entrance of Mayapan with the morning light gently spreading. (photo by Hana)

Figure 47 - Entering Mayapan 12-21-12 (photo by Hana)

Figure 48 - Group gathering at the entrance of Mayapan (photo by Hana)

≈ ≈ ≈

All the members of the group are now assembled at the entrance and we proceed in silence, as instructed, to the main pyramid. As the group meanders through the park I trail behind just feeling the energy of the morning light and the sites. I am taking in the sights, sounds, images, feelings, sensations, buildings, terrain and anything else consciously or subconsciously that will imprint this day in my memory. I want to feel and remember this day forever. Rounding the east side of the pyramid later than the main body of the group, I notice everyone gathering near a platform area that protrudes from the south east corner of the pyramid.

Figure 49 Mayapan December 21, 2012

The closer I get I am able to discern that an inner section of the
pyramid has been opened or excavated to reveal a three dimensional
relief on the wall. This must be the Condor and the Eagle that
ShavatY found in 2003. I snap a group photo from far away and then
move closer to join the group.

As I approach the relief, I catch my breath. What I see blows me
away. I can hardly describe the stunned sensation flowing through
me. I just stand and stare, frozen in my stance.

What I see is a depiction, an image, of what I felt in meditation this
morning when Eh HaY U and I connected during our ceremony.
During the ceremony I felt that I had left my head and went into my
heart. It was as if, in the connection with Eh HaY U, everything that
was in my head was drawn into the crystal skull and then moved
from the skull back into my heart upon the connection there. I felt as
if the space that had been my head was empty. Now I'm seeing those
sensations portrayed in the image before me. Chills run down my
neck and spine. I am stunned.

Figure 50 - Condor & Eagle Relief (photo by Brigitte)

I move closer to see the Condor on the left and on the right is the Eagle. In the middle is a human body with "no head". That's what I felt in meditation this morning; like the space where my head was became empty, a void, like I had no head. Now I'm standing in front of this drawing, thousands of years old, depicting an image of that feeling. I'm a bit shaky. Again I feel the chills run through my body. In the carving of the human, one sees a box or a square hole in the place where a head should be.

I'm now standing among our group watching ShavatY a few feet away up on the platform in front of the carving with Eh HaY U. The box opening in the area of the human head is about the size of Eh HaY U. I notice she is kneeling and has removed the crystal skull from the pink back pack and is doing a small invocation or inner ceremony she then rises and places Eh HaY U into the awaiting opening above the neck of the human form. She adjusts him right and left just slightly until she feels the energy click in. I sense this adjustment as she finds the right spot.

Figure 51 - Mayapan 12-21-12 preparing for reunification

Then very unexpectedly she announces that each of us should climb up onto the platform, enter behind the rope encasing the wall relief and connect with the energy of the relief while Eh HaY U is connected with it. This is completely unplanned. After connecting the skull and the relief ShavatY clearly gets the message that we each need to connect with it. We are each to face the relief with our arms spread out to the right and left with palms facing in. Then after a few seconds we are to turn around and place our back to the relief facing out in the same direction as the human with our arms spread wide palms out.

With the new laws in Mexico prohibiting ceremony at the pyramid parks we are pushing the envelope. However, to complete light work you do what you are guided to do. We are in the park before it's officially open and we are the only people in the park. We do however exercise caution by venturing up to the platform one at a time. In case anyone came around a single person could easily scamper down more easily unseen than a group of people which would likely draw attention.

Figure 52 - 12-21-12 connecting with the reunified Condor and Eagle (photo by Hana)

Figure 53 - Connecting with reunified energy (photo by Hana)

Figure 54 - Feeling the energy

Figure 55 - Mayapan 12-21-12 completing the reunification

Figure 56 - Mayapan 12-21-12 Task completed (photo by Hana)

Figure 57 - Mayapan 12-21-12 Double Helix energy (photo by Carolina)

One by one we connect with this amazing relief housing Eh HaY U in the box, the void where a head should be. On my turn, I lift myself up the short wall, walk across the rough uneven rocks and duck under the rope in front of the relief. First we, the relief and I, connect face to face and I can feel incredible energy from the connection. It feels as if it is pushing me back away from the wall as I face it. Next I turn around facing out in the same direction as the carving. In this position the energy is pulling me or sucking me back into the wall. We can stay only a few seconds each. It's difficult to pull away as I would like to experience this connection for longer. It is powerful and amazing.

One of our group, Myrtha, is upwards of eighty years and the last to connect. She connects from the platform edge, as it is too difficult for her to navigate over the rough rocks to directly touch the relief. We have done it. The healing and reunification of the Condor and the Eagle is complete.

Figure 58 - Condor, Eagle & Eh HaY U

≈ ≈ ≈

At this site, like yesterday at Uxmal, we are each given a piece of the ancient red corn. Again this is not for us to keep, but rather as a light worker to go out into this site, Mayapan, feel an energetic connection with it and offer this ancient knowledge, energy and connection back to Mother Earth. Again ShavatY reminds us that this corn carries sacred energy from all over the Americas from various shaman, elders and ceremonies. It is this energy that will be awakened now upon our sharing.

With my one kernel of the red corn and some of the white corn from the morning meditation, I venture off to follow my guidance and connect the sacred energies of the corn with this site. As I wander the grounds still glowing inside from the connection with Eh HaY U and the Eagle and the Condor, as well as our early morning ceremony, I see some brilliant blue flowers growing on the ground. I pick one to add to my offering as it reminds me of ShavatY's story this morning on the bus.

I pass over the cenote to the east of the pyramid. It has good energy, but it is not the spot. I read the sign. It says that they have columns inside the cenote opening and they did ceremony inside. Interesting, but still I don't feel drawn here. I continue walking with inner introspection and feel drawn to a hilltop (probably a mound of un-excavated ruins) with a collection of broken and partial ruins scattered at the top. I ascend the hill through a path of rock and leaves. I can tell the iguanas are here protecting the energy of the place. I can see the openings to their nests in between the rocks. Like Uxmal yesterday, these ancient guardians are here too.

Figure 59 - Animal like carving where I share my kernel

At the top I find a stone monument that was carved and resembled some kind of animal. There are iguana droppings on the carving and on the ground near it confirming that the guardians hang out here sunning themselves as they watch over the city. I sit on a piece of round column nearby and do a meditation connecting with the crystal skull energy of Mother Earth, to Mother Earth, to Father Sky and enter into the tiny space of the heart. I keep hearing birds behind me and to my left in the jungle.

At home I know the songs of most of the birds. The bird songs here are different, even exotic in an alluring way. At one point I feel guided to open my eyes and there are two large birds, possibly hawks, floating over the main pyramid where we just reunited the Condor and the Eagle. Although not an Eagle or a Condor, I suspect they felt the energy of the reunification and they came to represent the Condor and Eagle and the feathered serpent energy.

Figure 60 - Mayapan 12-21-12 Two birds over the pyramid after our ceremony (photo by Hana)

After meditation I leave my offering: the ancient piece of deep red corn, the blue flower, a small rose quartz and a piece of the white corn representing new energy on the carving of the animal as a gift to Mother Earth and to Mayapan.

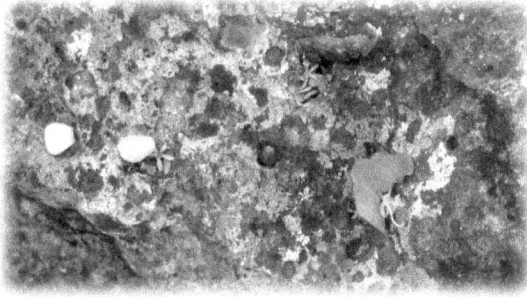

Figure 61 - white corn, rose quartz, red corn, and blue flower offering

I walk around and connect with other energies in the rooms, temples, observatory, and other buildings of Mayapan. The group is to gather for ceremony again in front of the main pyramid at 9:30am. It is nearing that time, and so I head to the main entrance to visit the "baño" before meeting up with the group.

Figure 62 - Bird carving at Mayapan

Figure 63 - Mayapan, Mayan glyph

Figure 64 - Mayapan wall 12-21-12 (photo by Hana)

Figure 65 - bird carvings at Mayapan (photo by Hana)

Figure 66 - Mayapan happy glyph

≈ ≈ ≈

As I re-enter the park after my visit to the ladies room, I make it only a few steps when I encounter several in our group flanking ShavatY wearing her now familiar pink backpack across her chest. My first thought is that they too are going to the ladies room before we meet for ceremony. I am a bit surprised when they share with me that we were finished here in Mayapan, and we will be gathering at the bus instead of the pyramid. I am a bit disappointed because I want to do the ceremony. However no worries, we are to do the ceremony later this evening at the hotel where we will connect to and set the vision for the coming age.

I do a one eighty about face and join ShavatY and her group walking in the direction from which I had just come, back in the direction of the bus. While walking I pose some questions that are on my mind to ShavatY.

"ShavatY, may I ask you a question about the ceremony at the relief?"

"Sure. What is it?" she responds.

"The box in the relief, the three dimensional opening where you placed Eh HaY U for the reunification on the pyramid wall, was that the purpose of the opening, the box? Was it built for that? Is its purpose to hold a crystal skull?"

ShavatY responds, "That is an excellent question. Yes, that is the purpose for the box to hold a crystal skull in ceremony. Not only is it the purpose, but also that purpose could only be fulfilled this day and this day only. The whole thing was built for this one day. For more than 26,000 years this has been its purpose."

She went on to say that you could have used it last week, yesterday, tomorrow or any other time and the energy, connection and power would not be there. This day and only this day was designated for its intended purpose. This day and this day only was when the inter-dimensional connection would work.

I am feeling shock at the answer, yet honored. I can feel the tears well up. To be given the gift of being present for the reunification of the Condor and the Eagle on this one very special day and to fulfill the purpose of Mayapan, to be part of it all is such an honor. How exciting to be involved with the ending of a cycle and the awakening of the new golden age to come. Whoever planned this obviously was at a very high level of consciousness to have been able to put this in place so long ago to be activated at this precise moment in time.

ShavatY continued explaining, they could and probably did use this site many times for ceremony, even crystal skull ceremony, but it didn't have the dimensional portal connection to the power on any other day except today.

≈ ≈ ≈

I feel so happy inside to be part of that. I am still digesting the enormity of it all as we re-board the bus. Shortly Carolina comes on the speaker and announces that she and ShavatY feel our mission and purpose here are complete. The feeling is that we were now being called to Merida to share our light there. Also the group is ready for coffee and some food and Merida will fulfill those needs for us and in return they will benefit from us sharing our light there.

Later tonight after our return to Izamal we will gather to do the ceremony at the hotel before going to dinner. The delayed ceremony feels right to me. Now Henry can join us too and be part of the completion energy and ceremony for December 21, 2012.

As the bus navigates the potholes in the dirt parking lot I pull my cell phone from its holster to check the time. It is 9:30am on 12/21/12 as we roll out of Mayapan. For many people the day is just beginning, but for me it feels like I have experienced a full day already, yet it's barely morning.

I take out my journal to make notes, however it sits in my lap as Mindy, my seatmate, and I talk and share experiences from the day. Several days later as I write this I can still recapture that peaceful feeling of awe that was draped over me during that morning ride to Merida.

I am torn between wanting to go back to the hotel and rest and check on Henry versus going to Merida. In a selfish way I don't want to go to Merida, into the city in among the noise and chaos and those disconnected from the energies of the enormous shift occurring around us. A saying is trying to surface in my mind... that which is shared freely becomes valuable and that which is guarded becomes obsolete. That is the essence, but not the exact wording. I can feel it at the edge of my mind.

What I am getting is that sharing these feelings we have been privileged to experience is our choice and to choose to share allows for the expansion of this energy. This reminds me of a Tibetan trained teacher of mine, Marcus Daniels. Marcus can both see and feel when someone drops into his or her heart.

I was in a heart-centering workshop with him several years ago. We were learning to drop into our hearts. As we sat in a circle, he was talking to the class. I was listening and I began to feel what he was saying and dropped into my heart without knowing I had done so. His acknowledgement to me that I had dropped into my heart was confirmation for me. That helped me know what it felt like as well as helped me recognize when I was there. Later that morning he again confirmed that I was in my heart, but then he questioned me as to why I wasn't sharing it.

Share it? Wow! I can consciously share heart space energy? I was so excited to learn that I "could" share. What a concept!

Now here in the Yucatan I have a reference for sharing the light, energies, love and connection we are experiencing with everyone and to start with that would be the people of Merida. As light workers and not just tourists the choice is made for us. It's off to Merida.

Figure 67 - Mayapan 12-21-12 early morning

Figure 68 - Mayapan (photo by Brigitte)

Figure 69 - Mayapan (photo by Brigitte)

Figure 70 - Mayapan

Figure 71 - Mayapan

Figure 72 - Mayapan (photo by Hana)

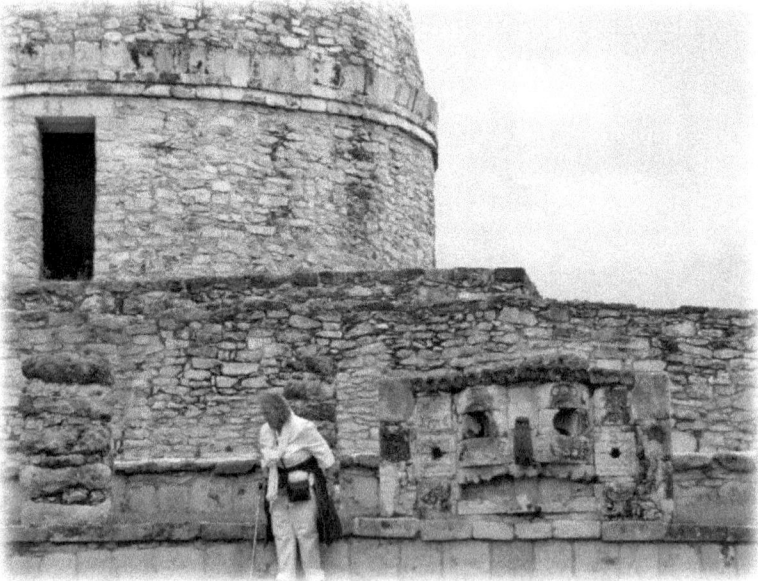

Figure 73 - Mayapan (photo by Brigitte)

Figure 74 - Mayapan (photo by Brigitte)

Figure 75 - Mayapan (photo by Hana)

Chapter 9 - Merida

December 21, 2012

We arrive to streets barricaded and lots and lots of soldiers and policemen peppering the throngs of people. The understanding in our group is that there are supposed to be some celebrations for December 21, 2012 going on in the main square. Carolina confirms a group reservation for lunch and then sets us free for a couple of hours to wander and explore.

Mindy, my New York City friend, and I break off and head into the square looking for coffee. As we are paying I ask the cashier, in Spanish, when the festivities will start?

She stops with her hand in mid-air holding our change and looks at me with a quizzical expression. "There are no festivities," she remarks. "The whole area is marked off because the El Presidente de Mexico is to appear there later today."

Ahhh…. now that could explain why Carolina was getting the hit to come to Merida and spread the new energies. The new president is pretty much universally despised. We've been hearing this since our arrival five days ago. This is also well documented in the news. I should mention here that Mexico recently "elected" a new president. The people feel the election was a mockery. Saying they are unhappy with the president is an understatement of great proportions. Cab drivers, waiters and other locals that we talked with had nothing good to say about the new president.

Mindy and I walk east into the main plaza with our coffee. The park fills the entire block with center of the park circular in nature with four streets bordering it: Calles 60 and 62 to the east and west and Calles 61 and 63 bordering it on the north and south. The metal barricade fencing surrounds the park and extends for a several blocks in every direction. Along Calle 61 on the north side of the park is the government building. Because of the President's visit there is metal fencing cordoning off the north side of the park into the center circle. The other three sides of the plaza are open to pedestrian traffic.

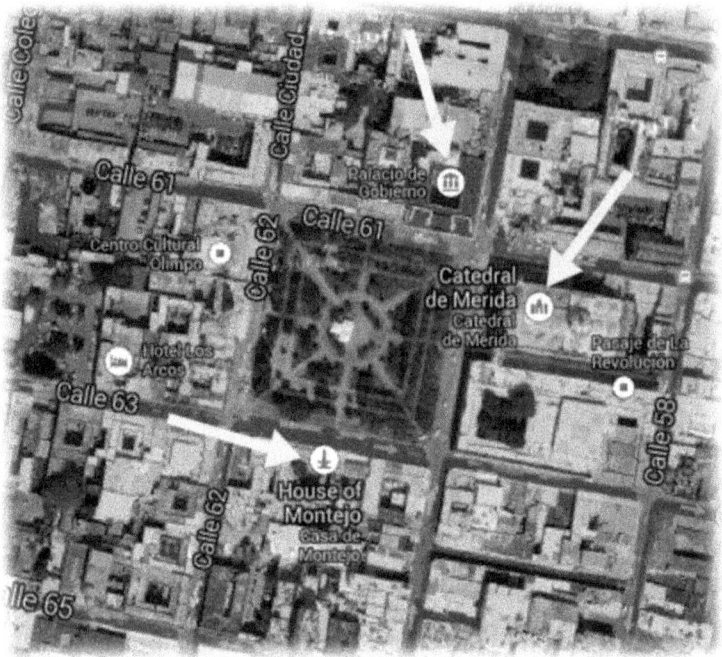

Figure 76 - Google Maps aerial of the central plaza in Merida

Figure 77 - North side of park - Government building (photo from Google maps)

Figure 78 - South side of park - House of Montejo (photo from Google maps)

Figure 79 - East side of park - Cathedral (photo from Google maps)

Figure 80 - West side of park - Independence Plaza (photo from Google maps)

We walk around feeling the energy. A small, stray, tan female pup comes up to Mindy and is sniffing her. The dog then runs into the center of the plaza where there are lots of pigeons, some small children laughing and playing and four protestors bearing bright fluorescent orange and fluorescent green poster board with hand written protests on them.

The four protestors in Merida are dressed like farmers or people from the rural areas. A few TV cameras are filming them. One lady with them is handing out flyers. A few people go up to talk with them or thank them. There are no chants, shouting or aggressiveness of any kind. It is all very peaceful. They are just there to deliver a message.

Figure 81 – Protesters (see oval) in the Plaza Merida December 21, 2012 (photo by Brigitte)

Meanwhile around them the children play, chasing the pigeons and laughing as they take flight and then land again. The stray pup can't resist and she too enters the plaza to stir up the pigeons by jumping in the air with them as they take flight. The pup returns to the pedestrian walk surrounding the center to connect again with Mindy and surprises her by jumping up to place her front paws on Mindy's waist. The dog must sense the energy she is carrying with her from Mayapan and the ceremonies earlier today.

Mindy and I head to the east edge of the plaza and cross the street to feel the energy in the four hundred and fifty plus year old cathedral. Many churches and power centers are built over ancient sacred sites so we want to feel this place.

Just as we turn to go Mindy says, "I feel like I want to go stand in the center of the plaza." She no more gets those words out of her mouth when she follows up with a negation of, "…Oh we can do that after the cathedral."

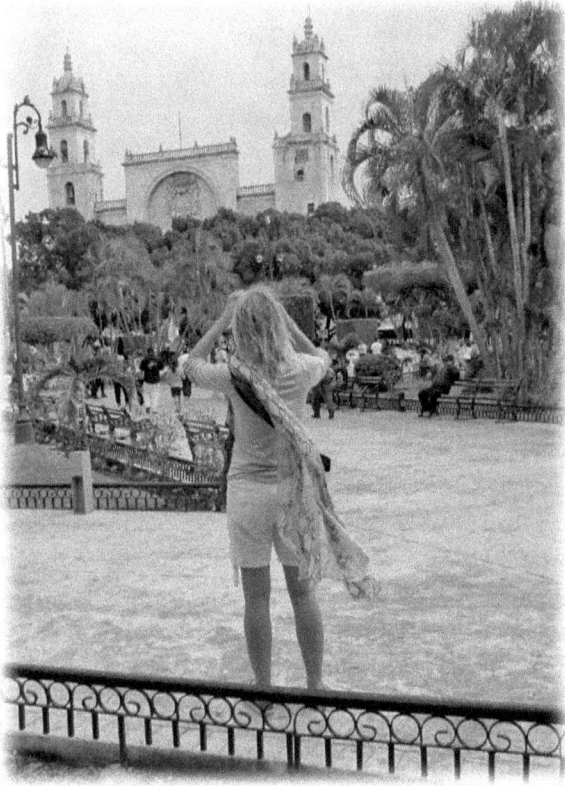

Figure 82 - Sophia snapping a photo of the cathedral (photo by Brigitte)

So off we go through the barricade border with security soldiers dotting the area. After crossing the street we enter the cathedral between two elderly Mexican ladies collecting donations and sitting on each side of the threshold at the entrance.

Inside we separate and I wander through taking notice of the architecture and looking for sacred geometry. There are circles within circles. There are curved arches and rounded columns. There are many rounded shapes including the center dome. In sacred geometry the circle and curves represent the feminine and straight lines and angles represent the masculine. The church feels masculine to me, but looking around I sense that the creators intended it to be very feminine. Maybe the feminine geometry is there to balance out the masculine energy of the church and the priests. It's a possibility.

At the rear of the church I looked up at the center dome from an angle versus directly under the dome. From this vantage point one of the naves/arches intersects with my view of the dome creating a vesica piscis: the shape of the intersection of two circles when they overlap; the fundamental root of sacred geometry; the place of power and creation, not above, not below, but rather in both locations at once. I soak this in for a while.

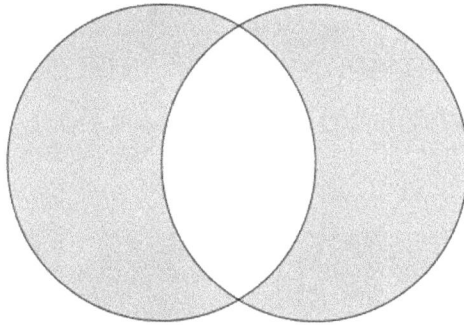

Figure 83 - Vesica Picis (image from Wikipedia)

Soon Mindy and I meet up near the rear and exit. As we leave I drop all of my change into the two containers of the elderly women flanking the threshold. It's time to share and spread the new energies of this new age in many ways, including financially.

Figure 84 - Merida 12-21-12 Plaza Grande (photo by Brigitte)

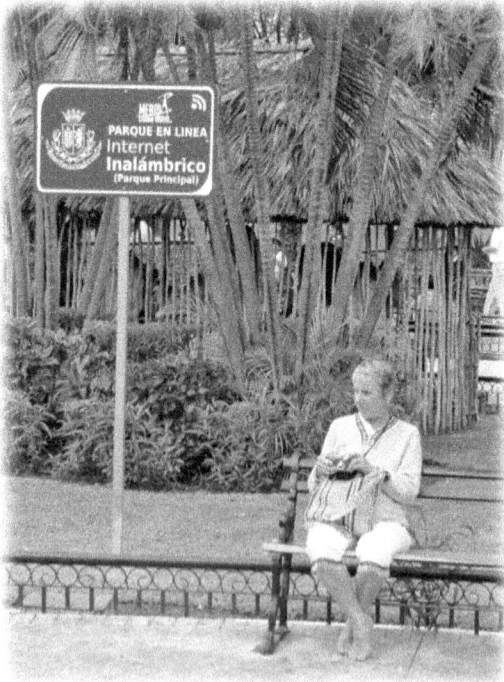

Figure 85 - Merida 12-21-12 (photo by Brigitte)

Crossing the street back to the plaza I stop and ask a soldier when the president is arriving. He responds that he is not sure but he believes around 4:30pm or 5:00pm. It is just before noon; although having woken up at 2:30am it feels as if it is a different day. Our group will leave Merida after lunch so we will not be in town for the presidential visit. Given the country's animosity towards their new leader it is no wonder our group was drawn here to connect and spread our love and energies even though officially the new era won't dawn until tomorrow (but over a span of 13,000 years we're close enough). Today is the last day of the 5th world of the Maya, December 21, 2012.

Back in the plaza, Mindy and I begin making our way into the center of the center circle to fulfill Mindy's earlier desire. We get within fifteen feet of the center of the center and we both stop as if we can go no further. The energy has changed. The children are gone. The pigeons are gone. The stray pup is gone. What remains are the protestors peacefully holding their signs. We try to move forward, but feel frozen to our spot.

Not successful in moving forward into the center we change direction and cross the street to the south side of the plaza. Here we find the exterior of a building (the House of Montejo) very intriguing with ornate statuesque reliefs bordering each window as well as along the roofline. Inside we are disappointed to find it to be shops, offices and a bank.

Figure 86 - House of Montejo roofline carvings

Figure 87 - House of Montejo window detail

Exiting we begin to study the building's face. I become fascinated. Just under the roof line spaced a few feet apart facing down is an entire row of three-dimensional pinecones. Pinecones represent both the Fibonacci sequence in sacred geometry and the pineal gland and third eye energy. Underneath that, on the face of the building, is a row of molding with three-dimensional figurines running the entire length of the building, similar to crown molding. They are strange creatures. I can't decide if they are dragons or dogs. They have very thin bodies with ribs showing and are facing each other in pairs. In the middle of each pair is an angel.

Coming down from the roofline closer to street level flanking the enormous windows are carvings of a female on the left and a male on the right. Each wears a crown over their third eye. Each has a free-swinging torch on the left. Where the legs would be is a trapezoid shape with intersecting circles getting smaller as they go down and the narrowing face. The top circle or disk has a line wrapped around with the loose end extending down through each circle. When you followed this line to the bottom the end of the line holds a pendulum.

Figure 88 - House of Montejo

I am completely fascinated with the carvings on the exterior of this building and all the symbology that is hiding within plain site. People walking by are barely taking notice. What influence could all this symbology have on their subconscious? Who created this? Did they plan for it to be an influence? Did they intend for it to be a message? Was it a code to be decoded? Would initiates be able to extract meanings? My mind and heart have connected here and are full of awe and questions. I snap a couple of photos to view later at home on my computer to study the detail.

Mindy & I again cross the street into the plaza once again and go our separate ways to make an offering to Mother Earth of the white corn from this morning's ceremony. I find a tree that calls to me. I ask permission to make an offering. I ask that the energies of this dawning new age be received here in this location to help the wisdom of Mother Earth to come forward and awaken the people who populate this plaza so that they too may remember as this new age dawns.

That completed we begin to head west to exit the plaza when we encountered another group of our traveling companions. ShavatY was in the middle with her pink pack hanging over her abdomen holding the crystal skull, Eh HaY U and four others from the group with her. We speak about the President coming and the protestors in the center. ShavatY heads right to the center to speak with the protestors. I follow trying to read the signs, but don't comprehend their message with my rusty Spanish. When I look back I see that Mindy still can't enter the center as if being held back by some unseen energy.

Later that evening I speak with ShavatY about the protestors, and she explains how the people who where there were very brave. One of our members commented that there were TV cameras there and that the protestors would receive publicity for their cause.

"No," responded ShavatY, "that footage will be used by the government to identify them and their families and possibly harass them (cause them suffering) for their protests. They are vey brave people."

ShavatY had asked the protesters why there were not more there to protest. They told her that they were very poor and they could only come up with the money for these four to travel. Being from the USA I did not fully appreciate their courage and bravery for voicing their truth. I took it as a common right rather than the brave act that it was.

Figure 89 - Merida 12-21-12 Shoeshine

Leaving the plaza again we pass Karl at the shoe shine stand receiving attention to his shoes that had been traveling for three weeks from Peru to Bolivia and now the Yucatan. After an exchange we continue on with Sue from Australia in her bare feet. I have yet to see her in shoes. It's as if she is full of aboriginal blood and on an amazing walk about. We stopped to read the sign over the municipal building bordering the west side of the plaza. The name was in the center of the sign and to my surprise each of the corners is decorated with the all seeing eye; the eye of Ra. Imagine that finding an Egyptian symbol in this small town in the northern Yucatan, go figure.

Chapter 10 – Izamal and the Closing Ceremony

December 21, 2012

After lunch our group walk backs the few blocks through the barricades to the parking lot and the bus for our ride back to Izamal. On the bus back, Carolina announces that on Saturday morning, tomorrow, there will be a sunrise service with Hunbatz Men, a Mayan elder, about a half hour ride from the hotel. She told us to think about if we wish to go, and later at dinner she will check with us and confirm who wants to attend and what time the bus will leave.

Hunbatz Men is probably the most widely known Mayan Elder as he is the most public. Because of that he is the one that most foreigners connect with first when they come to the Yucatan. He is a member of the Itza Maya council of elders. He started the Mayan Ceremonial, Cultural and Educational Center in Lol Be (not far from Chichen Itza). In 2011 he became widely known for his crystal skull journey across America. He started in New York City on October 26, 2011 and ended with a ceremony in Los Angeles on 11-11-11. You can look him up on youtube.com and view lots of personal videos from this journey.

≈ ≈ ≈

Upon our arrival in Izamal, Henry is there in the lobby to greet us feeling much better. He's happy to see all our shining faces and anxious to hear all about our day. Everyone scatters for a little rest before we meet at 6:30pm for the December 21, 2012 closing meditation.

Tomorrow after our visit to Chichen Itza some of our group will begin to depart for home or other travels. Miryam & Bonnie will head back to California and Myrtha, our grandmother, who has been traveling with the December 6 group, will continue her adventure to Ecuador and then to Tucson in February for the annual rock and gem show in the dessert. What an amazing lady. I admire her stamina and her sense of adventure. What this means is that tonight is our last night together as a group.

I have with me gifts that I brought from home; some Emerald gemstones and Emerald Isle, NC magnetic book marks for everyone. I have been carrying them with me to all the sites and ceremonies on this trip, so they have collected the energies, love, awakenings, etc. of our travels. I want to wrap them and gift them to our companions, but I also would like to have a short rest since I had very little sleep last night before the 2:30am morning wake up call this morning. Henry volunteers to venture into town to find some gift-wrapping paper.

Henry, who speaks only a few words of Spanish, is instructed to purchase "papel de navidad" (Christmas paper). He strolls into town and after no luck finding it in several stores he encounters a store attended by four teenage girls who speak only Spanish. Through constant giggles and speaking different languages the girls manage to supply him not only with a small roll of paper but also the tape to complete the wrapping. Twenty-three wrapped packages and a shower later we head to the pavilion to gather for the closing ceremony for December 21, 2012.

≈ ≈ ≈

A 6:30pm we gather in the pavilion between the grassy area of the hotel and the pool for a closing ceremony with ShavatY and Eh HaY U before heading off to dinner. ShavatY has the altar set up including a single bowl of white corn, the remnants from the four bowls this morning. Gosh was that just this morning? It feels as if it could have been days ago.

Forming a circle our worldwide group gathers around the altar. ShavatY tells how she feels we need this closure to our work today. She explains how working with Eh HaY U is a two way street and this step will help us integrate, solidify and plant our energies and desires for the new world to come. Eh HaY U was helped by us in the ceremonies and in turn he is helping us in our awakenings.

Crystal skulls work on multi-dimensional levels, most of which we are not aware of, but are affected by just the same. As one gazes into the skull different effects are felt and received during different light settings: daylight, darkness and with a mechanical light shining through at different angles.

So tonight as we meditate, ShavatY walks around Eh HaY U shining a flashlight through his beautiful clear crystal structure so we can all see, receive and perceive his multi-dimensional energy from many angles. Once we feel the energies strongly we are to close our eyes and perceive the light through our closed eyes.

We are at the threshold of creating a new era for the next 26,000 years. What do we see for the coming times? What do we want to create for this new age to come? We are invited to send out our creations tonight through Eh HaY U.

As ShavatY begins circling the altar shining a flashlight through the beautiful crystal, I close my eyes and perceive from there and enter into my heart. I begin to feel this new age that is coming. As I do I sense, see and feel in my inner vision many things.

I feel and see a life without a monetary system that eliminates the divide between the have and the have-nots. I see, sense and feel a world where there is truly freedom to learn and grow. A place where each new baby is watched to recognize the gifts they bring and they are consistently encouraged to know and fulfill their purpose. Where everyone feels their inner connection and a knowingness that we are one and connected to all.

A place where Mother Nature is respected and honored. A place where she is our teacher and our giver of sustenance and healing. A place where true leaders are in place and politics no longer exists. Certain persons are groomed for true heart based leadership from birth.

I envision a place where talents for everyone of all ages are recognized, cultivated and encouraged. Where contributions to society are not based on monetary return, but rather overall betterment. Where leaders decide things based on the good for all and the effects things have on our beautiful planet for many, many generations to come.

A place where love is felt between strangers. A place of peace and safety. A place where communication is heart based and unspoken rather than duality head based and spoken with untruths and hidden meanings. Where language is perceived on sensory levels from the heart not verbal levels from the head.

A thriving planet easily supporting a thriving creative society. A place where art is highly valued and strongly encouraged. Where creativity and imagination are more cherished than even sports heroes and movie stars of today.

One where mechanical vehicles will be an ancient memory and travel will come from our own light bodies. Healing will be from Mother Earth substances rather than synthetic drugs. Healing will be heart centered and energy based. Healing will come from maintaining a clear body always with little to no need of healing for there will be virtually no disease. An abundant future without energy needs such as electricity and gasoline that people pay for, but rather harnessing the free energies from the vacuum available to all.

The images, sensations, and feelings flow easily. Describing them adequately is more difficult. Hopefully you get the sense of the themes that came to me.

Here we are in a small group in the northern Yucatan helping to create a vision of the future for the next 26,000 years. Twenty three people from various parts of the world have come together to create ceremony and visions for our new world to come and to return home carrying this energy and spreading the seeds in the many places we call home. Our group is but one of hundreds that are gathered in the Yucatan today, one of thousands that are gathered around the globe creating our world to come.

ShavatY invites us yet again to take some of the white corn, the symbol of the new world energies coming forth, home with us to do ceremony especially between now the birthing of this new energy today at the winter solstice and March 21, 2013, the spring equinox. March 21, 2013 is the balancing point of this new energy birthed during the shortest day of the year in darkness and it will stretch and awaken from now until March 21, 2013. "Take the white corn, go home and do ceremony with it where you live," said ShavatY. "Contribute to the balancing of this new energy."

Chapter 11- Walk to Dinner

December 21, 2012

After closing ceremony we file out of the hotel for our walk to dinner. Henry and I end up at the back of the pack with Brigitte and Sophia, the two young ladies we met the very first day at the Marriott waiting for the bus to collect us. As we walk and chat about the day the conversation turns to our afternoon in Merida. Sophia and Brigitte were the last to join us for lunch, almost an hour later than the appointed noon meeting time. Sophia has wandered off from the group to do some energy cleaning on several occasions, so I was not surprised to hear that the reason they were late for lunch was that they were clearing energy. However as we continue our walk, an amazing story unfolds.

Earlier today in Merida, Sophia and Brigitte are drawn to the cathedral from the central plaza with clouds blanketing the sky. As they enter the church mass is in progress. Sophia feels the energy is dark and heavy in the church. Without knowing it Brigitte too feels the same and she also is cleaning the energy in her way. So both of them are cleaning energy unbeknownst to each other. As the mass nears its end, the priest invites all the church guests to exchange greetings and shake hands. Brigitte and Sophia welcome the opportunity and use it to spread their love and energy among everyone they greet and touch.

[*Later I learn from each of them separately, that they feel they opened a portal of light that was located in the energetic space of the church. (This makes sense since most churches are built over sacred sites.)   Brigitte feels they connected the church with the new unity consciousness grid; the grid that was completed in February of 2008 and took 13,000 years to accomplish.*]

Upon moving to the center of the church to meet and greet she sees a massive Jesus on a cross bearing a sign stating "Made in Minnesota USA" and underneath the cross bar she reads "Christo en Unidad"

(Christ in Unity). They exit the church and looked into the sky and the blue was breaking through the clouds, but just in the sky right over the church roof with the clouds parting at the center of the church. They take this sign as a confirmation that they have connected the church back to the light consciousness of the Unity Consciousness grid surrounding the earth.

They cross the street at the corner of Calles 60 and 61, which leads them to the government building rather than into the park. At this point, neither of them has any knowledge that the President is coming to town today. They still hold the belief that the plaza is cordoned off for the December 21, 2012 celebration festivities, like we were told on the bus. It is about 2 hours later, when they arrive for lunch that they hear about the presidential visit.

A soldier on guard at Calle 61 asks them if they want to enter the building.

"Yes," they said. In they go innocent of the knowledge of today's upcoming visitor.

Once inside the government building the pair proceeds to the second floor. As they are standing in front of a large locked conference room, along comes another soldier asking if they would like to see inside.

"Of course. Yes, we would."

The soldier (angel as Brigitte describes him) unlocks the door, turns on the lights and tells them to look around and for them to take as long as they like.

There in front of them is massive and extremely long conference table surrounded by chairs except at the head of the table where a chair is sitting on top of the table. Brigitte says to Sophia, "Take my picture sitting in that chair on top of the table."

Sophia, soft in nature, sternly responds, "No. You cannot. The energy in here is black. We must clean it."

Brigitte whose role in life is the catalyst that initiates the actions of others has again initiated something in Sophia. The two of them just met only three days ago, but given all they've shared since then it feels as if they've known each other years instead of days.

Back in the conference room set for a formal meeting, lights on and door open Sophia begins to clean the room while Brigitte holds the energy, holds the space. [*During the walk to the restaurant that night they individually share with me that they could not have done it without the other. Brigitte tells me she does not believe she could have cleared the energy of the room herself. And Sophia shares how her work was not possible without Brigitte there to hold the energy.*]

Sophia walks around the conference room cleaning and taking on the black energy she sees and feel. She then leaves the room and clears the energies from her bodies. She returns to the conference room two more times to clean and clear until she feels complete. Her confirmation that her work has been accomplished and that it is effective awaits her upon exiting the government building. The sky is clear and blue over the building.

The rest of the group has ordered lunch and some are even eating by the time the duo joins us. All is well. They quickly place their order and conversation begins. It is here and now they learn that they have just cleared the conference room where the President of Mexico will gather later this day December 21, 2012.

While this story unfolds Sophia and I have drifted to the rear of the pack. Everyone has gone ahead to the restaurant including Henry and Brigitte. During the journey Sophia pauses in the middle of the street several times so into telling her story, oblivious to the rest of the world around her. I let her story unfold as I watch for and protect us from cars and motorcycles passing by. Several times I steer us around potholes and at other times I gently urge her to move on. The sky has darkened and the group is nowhere in sight in front of us. It is an incredible sharing that takes place on the way to the restaurant. I feel very privileged to hear it straight from Sophia and

Brigitte mere hours after their experience while the glow of the energy and experience is still upon them.

Eventually I look up to see both Henry and Brigitte back tracking in the dark from the restaurant to find us and to make sure we were ok. There is no hint of concern on my part. I feel surrounded and protected by light during the whole walk even though we are not traversing the best of neighborhoods. Henry and Brigitte seeing that we were fine and making progress, albeit slow, disappear again into the restaurant as Sophia and I bring up the rear completing the gathering.

Chapter 12 - Dinner and Gifts

December 21, 2012

Inside the restaurant I am greeted by a surprise. Another December 2012 group led by a friend of Carolina has joined us and we are now five tables of guests. With Christmas gifts wrapped for our group only I now circulate the tables and deliver a gift to each of our group from Henry and me. Upon completion I look around to find Henry so I may join him for dinner seating. There he is at the last table with ShavatY and Carolina and no one else. So I go and join the three of them for dinner.

Henry orders a bottle of red wine and we all have a glass with dinner. He is anxious to hear about the day so the three of us take turns telling him things that occurred.

≈ ≈ ≈

As dinner arrives I find myself in conversation with ShavatY. I share with her my surprise at the intensity of emotions during the Condor and the Eagle ceremony this morning, how I was not prepared for how deeply it affected me. I knew it would be emotional, but not to the extent that I experienced.

She explains that many factors came into play this morning including: the location, Mayapan, being in alignment with the pyramid and being there at 5:11am (11:11am universal time) on this date, December 21, 2012, the end of the Mayan calendar. Not only was all of that in play to create the emotion we felt and the healing energy, but also each of the participants was fulfilling his or her own destiny which brought in another whole level and dimension to the ceremony.

Fulfilling our destiny? That's powerful. I hadn't looked at it that way. I knew I felt a strong pull to be here. I had airplane tickets to Pittsburgh already booked and changed my plans because I felt such a strong urge to be with like-minded folks doing ceremony at this incredible time. I hadn't thought of that, but it makes sense after hearing others in the group tell of how they too were drawn to come. I was drawn to this particular tour out of many on the internet. Guidance was coming from somewhere to draw me here.

Inside I feel a click, like when you hear truth and it makes sense or when something naturally falls into place. I'm blessed to be here. I give thanks for the guidance that brought me here.

ShavatY goes on to say that the whole complex was built for this day. Thousands of years ago they began preparing for this day. They knew we would come.

≈ ≈ ≈

Carolina does the rounds with the tables to confirm who is participating in the sunrise service tomorrow, December 22, 2012 the first day of the new cycle. After getting the count she discusses this with our driver then announces that we are to be on the bus at 4:45am for the ceremony with Hunbatz Men. Ah, that means waking up at 4:15am versus 2:30am. Just the sound of it feels like sleeping in. Henry and I are both on board for attending the ceremony.

We begin our journey back to the hotel for rest. The restaurant staff directs us to walk home via town rather than the way we came. Good thing. In the dark I'm not sure I could find my way back meandering through the neighborhood. About a dozen of us stroll back to the hotel laughing and talking. We stop at the horse drawn carriage vendor and bargain for a ride from the plaza to our hotel. In the end we decide we're too tired to enjoy it tonight. In high spirits we arrive back at our hotel and settle in for some well-deserved sleep.

Chapter 13 – Lol Be The 13th Flower of Life

December 22, 2012

Fast asleep I'm startled to waking by Henry saying, "It's time to get up." Before I can even sit up, he recants and says, "Oh no, it's not time yet. It's only midnight."

From then until 3:45am I wake up several times. Finally I fall asleep assuring myself not to worry, because we have two alarms set.

At 4:39am, twenty-four minutes past both alarms, I bolt out of bed announcing, "We're late!"

Some how both smart phone alarms were set, but the sound was off so neither of them rang. Having showered and set everything out last night, I quickly dress in my clothes that are laid out on the extra bed. Hurriedly I brush my teeth and leave Henry getting ready as I rush to the lobby.

Scurrying down the path day bag over my shoulder, I pass Carolina and tell her that we overslept.

"Don't worry. There is no rush. The bus is ready. We'll wait for Henry," comes Carolina's calm and dismissive reply of a seasoned tour leader.

Shortly all are gathered and the bus pulls out loaded with a quiet group nodding off as we roll away into the black morning.

About twenty minutes past 5:00am in the heavy dark our bus pulls up in front of an entrance marked with a large white rock painted with the words LOL BE 13th Flower of Life. Our party spills out of the bus into the cold dark morning. Hunbatz Men, the Mayan Elder who owns this complex, greets us with his shock of white hair and a cup of coffee in his hands (boy would hot coffee taste good right now). He directs our driver where to park the bus. No sooner had our party descended our bus when another bus pulls up and the gathering throng grows larger. Next a few cars and another bus arrive.

With the crowd swelling Hunbatz gathers everyone together and instructs us to stay on the pathway. Do not go off into the trees on either side. Stay on the marked road he commands. We are to follow him to the white private home about one hundred meters in the distance. There are about forty to fifty people in the group huddled closely together to stave off the morning's chill, to keep to the path's center and to stay within the glow of the one flashlight present. We head north into the darkness. About a third of the way there we meet a couple with a foot long LED light illuminating the rock-lined path. The couple speaks to Hunbatz in Spanish and then leaves to bring up the rear or escort latecomers. I'm not sure.

Figure 90 - Hunbatz Men

Our collection of bodies continues north following Hunbatz. In about four minutes the outline of the white stucco home appears. As we grow near I see there are others already there. Our group snakes onto the porch joining them under the dark canopy of a cloudless sky filled with stars. The open-air porch is wide and stretches the entire length of the home and is surrounded by a short concrete wall painted red. Hunbatz instructs someone to count our numbers. Curious, I watch and listen. We are currently sixty-eight strong on this beautiful morning.

The house faces south looking down the pathway from where we arrived. Henry, me, Mindy, Brigitte, Sophia, Miryam and a few others from our group are there at the east end of the porch. Our group has become co-mingled with the other groups. Jupiter is glowing brightly behind me in the eastern sky. To my right hovering over the roof of the house the big dipper, Ursa Major, is glowing.

Henry takes his compass out of his backpack and confirms that the star at the edge of the cup of the dipper is indeed pointed directly north.

Inside I feel anticipation and excitement. Today is the first day of the new age, the first day of the Mayan 6th world. A new 5,125-year cycle begins today and the start of a 26,000-year cycle. We are in alignment with the center of the galaxy for the first time in 26,000 years. Plus, the 13,000-year female cycle will dawn this morning.

I can feel her. I can feel her dawning this day. I can feel her awakening after 13,000 years of sleep.

I can hear music from the other side of the porch. With the crowd growing I cannot see them, but the sounds of a guitar and a flute float in the air. The anticipation grows. New comers are arriving continuously. We are nearly ninety in number now. Hunbatz is speaking. He is telling us that we are on private property. This is important since the government has banned all Maya, and everyone else, from performing ceremony at any of the government owned sacred sites. Hunbatz continues, "On this land is a Mayan stele; a stele with the date December 22, 2012 on it; the date of the first day of the new cycle."

My body is covered with chills. I had no idea. Again I feel honored to be here on this first day to welcome the goddess energy into the new age. There are tears in my eyes. I let the emotions flow as I feel the beauty surrounding me under this canopy of stars on this dark and chilly morning.

Hunbatz goes on to say that a Mayan crystal skull, Kin-Batz, is being returned to the Mayans in today's ceremony. Soon on his signal we will proceed back down the path to the south. When we do, the first in line will be Hunbatz followed by the French couple, Carole Tridon and Francke Echardour the caretakers of Kin-Batz, then the Mayan musicians. Behind them he asks that we form two lines, the one on the left will be the women and the right line will be populated by the men. This formation is so that the women will be in the front when the procession ends and the men in back; a physical representation and commemoration of the feminine cycle that is being birthed.

Time passes and the glow of pre-dawn light begins saturating the sky. It is difficult now to see the dipper. Bright Jupiter is still shining, but now against a gray blue. I feel her, the feminine energy; she's stretching and awakening. The tipping point is here, a slight edge to the female energy for the first time in 13,000 years. It will take nine years for this new female energy to fully awaken and emerge. Today she feels so happy and joyful. She knows we are here to celebrate her awakening today. I feel as if I've already received a blessing; if I receive nothing more today I will still feel complete.

The numbers continue growing as new comers keep appearing from the path. By my count we are now over one hundred and nineteen. I'm getting anxious as movement and posturing begins at the porch steps. It's almost time.

Figure 91 - Lol Be complex entrance

Many of the arrivals are wearing all white for ceremony. As another small group of eight or ten gathers in the yard flanking the steps of the overflowing porch, I see someone who looks familiar. How strange, yet this person reminds me of Conchita, the teacher and teacher instructor for Drunvalo Melchizedek. I met her in Sedona in May when I attended the Awakening the Illuminated Heart workshop there for five days. She and her partner, Lorena sat in the front row assisting Drunvalo that week. However it is not likely to be Conchita since her home is on the other side of Mexico, over 2000 kilometers and more than twenty hours away. How synchronistic it would be to meet her here, if that is she.

≈ ≈ ≈

A buzz in the air accompanies the parade as the procession begins. The throng spills off the porch and forms two lines walking south along the same path from which we arrived. The flute music from the Mayan musicians fills the air as we move along. About two thirds of the way back to the entrance of Lol Be, Hunbatz moves off the path onto a cement platform on the left. The platform holds the stele bearing today's date, December 22, 2012 in Mayan glyphs.

Many are still very far back and feeling the destination has been reached some begin to step off the path to get a better vantage point. We are again asked to stay within the path for a couple of reasons: 1. Not to disturb the animals and 2. So as not to harm the many young fruits and vegetables planted. At this point the line of two by two begins to break apart and a mass of bodies grows around the stele platform area. Men and women become intermingled, no longer in separate organized lines.

I see a member of our group in the front row take her crystal skull up to the altar and place him at the base of the stele next to Kin Batz, one of the thirteen Mayan crystal skulls. His caretakers, Carole and Francke, who led today's procession, are returning him to the Mayan people. Other individuals from the crowd begin to place crystals and stones on, near, and around the base of the stele.

As this is happening Hunbatz instructs the facilitators to arrange the crowd into two lines facing the platform where the ceremony is going to take place with the women in front and the men behind.

Quite content, I wait where I am without moving forward as I feel I've gotten so much already just being here as the light awakens. I don't need to be front and center. Soon others are telling all the women to move to the front and then in a group behind them the men. It is the feminine age and he is starting this ceremony by honoring the women and asking them to come to the front. There are two men in front of me with their video cameras at the ready to record the ceremony and they obviously don't want to move from their perceived choice spot. A woman beside me tries to move forward past them and explains that the women are to move up front.

"No," one the two responds, "women in the first row and men in the second row. We are in the second row."

It matters not to me that I stand behind them. I'll get whatever I'm here for from wherever I stand.

Soon more and more women are moving forward and the men behind. A man comes up behind me and reaches his arm past me to tap the two men who are now surrounded by a sea of women and says to them, "Come on." Then he motions with a tilt of his head to the back of the crowd.

As I turn to look in the direction of his head motion, I see all the men are at the rear, on the west side of the path, and all the women are at the front, the east side of the path except for these two. The two lone males finally acquiesce and retreat to the west with the rest of the males.

Figure 92 - Lol Be stele 12-22-12

Crystals continue to be passed forward and placed up front for the ceremony. Mine are all in my backpack. They are here at the ceremony. They are picking up the energy. I don't feel compelled to place them at the altar.

As the women gather closer I turn to my right and find myself face to face with Conchita. That was her I saw from the porch before the procession started. I introduce myself and tell her we met in

Sedona in May at the workshop. I also share that I was just accepted earlier this month for the Awakening the Illuminated Heart teacher's training in April 2013 which she coordinates and co-presents with Drunvalo.

She greets me and introduces me to her daughter and a couple of others translating into Spanish that I will be joining them in Chapala for training. The smiles are dawning on their faces as our eyes meet in greeting. At that moment her assistant, Lorena, joins the group and recognizes me from my picture in my teacher training application. Lorena tells Conchita this in Spanish. Conchita relays the message to me in English. I share that I remember her as well from Sedona. We exchange smiles and greetings. Inside I feel this unexpected meeting is a confirmation that my decision to apply for teacher training is indeed the path for me at this time.

[*Months later I learn that Conchita was there leading a travel group for One Heart Productions.*]

≈ ≈ ≈

The ceremony begins and Hunbatz's messages are spoken in Spanish and translated into other languages by participants and group leaders. Some parts of the ceremony are delivered first in Spanish and then repeated in English.

Figure 93 - Carole & Francke with the first rays of sun shining over their shoulders 12-22-12

Hunbatz is saying that the Maya start counting the new calendar, the new cycle, the new world with the dawn of the first day. Soon the sun will rise. Go within and feel the energy of the sun as it rises and shines on your face. This is the start of a new world, a world where the feminine energy will emerge.

As he speaks I look around to drink in my surroundings and feel the shifting that is occurring symbolized today with the females in front and the males behind. Except Sophia, she's among the men. I call to her, as does someone else simultaneously. She hears and moves forward with the women.

Hunbatz is now talking about how the Maya have lost their knowledge. He says that their memories were erased by the conquistadors through the destruction of their codices (folding books) and other sacred items over time. Here in Lol Be, a private complex, the Mayan will start to recreate their knowledge. They will have a school here. They will start to relearn what they once knew. This small parcel, Lol Be the 13th Flower of Life, will be used to train, to learn and to reconstruct.

The French couple, Carole and Francke, is here to begin that process. Hunbatz continues telling us that on this day our knowledge is being returned via their gift of the crystal skull, Kin Batz. After today it will go to a museum in Merida for a few months and then it will be returned to the Maya at Palenque. The couple then spoke of their honor in being the keepers of the skull, where it had been, and how they know Kin Batz is ready to come back to the Maya.

Carole, reads a poem in Spanish for the dedication and return of the skull to the Maya. I close my eyes as she reads it. With my rusty Spanish I understand very little however, I feel its beauty. I feel the love in the message. I feel the warmth of the sunshine on my face and I'm open as I listen. Suddenly an energy surge comes at me. It is like the rush of colors on Star Trek when they go into hyper drive, although it is not fast. It enters into me and merges into my head. I am surprised and taken aback; even physically I am moved backwards a half step upon receiving this energy. I have no idea what it means. It felt positive and empowering is all I can tell you. Blue is the most predominant color I remember. I would love to find a copy of this poem, as it was truly beautiful.

[Months later searching for a copy of this message I connect on facebook with Conchita who gave me an address for Hunbatz; I sent

*an email to Hunbatz Men; and I found a link to **www.kin-batzgate.com**. Eventually I did indeed make a connection with Carole Tridon. Upon explaining that I was seeking a copy of her message to include in this book she graciously emails me a copy in English.*

Much to my surprise I found out it is not a poem at all, but rather a channeling that came to her on 12-12-12 for the purpose of being shared on December 22, 2012 during the ceremony at Lol Be. The channeling is from Pacal Votan, the ruler-king from 603-683 BC in the glorious city of Palenque in Chiapas, Mexico.

Figure 94 - image of sarcophagus lid of Pacal Votan

Many of you may be familiar with the image of the elaborately carved lid of his sarcophagus found at Palenque. This image was made famous by Erich von Daniken in his book, "Chariots of the Gods? Unsolved Mysteries of the Past," published in 1968. Today many debate if this image does or does not depict Pacal Votan commandeering some type of craft or vehicle.]

I express my gratitude here to Carole for permission to share this channeling here in its entirety.

≈ ≈ ≈

Pacal Votan's message for the 12/22/12

"Imanna, write for the people of the Earth the words I am telling you.
Children of the Earth, Soul friends,
Finally, the time has come to speak to you.

Never before did I express myself through a channel. I chose this one
to convey to you
The important message for these changing times.

You are at the dawn of joyful events, and soon
The coming of the Wise shall take place.
Be courageous until the day of the Return of the Ancients.

Many of you gather this day
To merge the light of your heart
Together with the dance of the stars.
You, the People of the Earth,
Are the chosen ones
To anchor in the light of heaven.

Your decision to incarnate at this memorable time
Is such that you have chosen to be
The architects of the Terra Nova.
Your determination to reveal
The sacred in all things is
Your gateway to heaven revealed.

Once, when I ruled Palenque
My territory was prosperous
And also included Beings from elsewhere
Who came from the stars,
As it was also in glorious Egypt, and Tibet.
We were still under the reign of powerful advanced beings
Who came to help us in our humanity.

Now the time for help has come in turn.
For you are ruled by beings
With no great cosmic consciousness,
Barely a planetary consciousness,
And all of us, together, through our light thoughts
Need to send them our support
So they allow themselves to be carried by the change
That is underway in the consciousness of humanity.

My everlasting friends, enlightened souls
You need to carry with your crystal hearts all that is in the shadows
and in oblivion.
The darkness will fight, trying to resist,
Also you should pray harder,
And in the coming months,
Be centered in your crystal hearts.
Be aware that the passage has begun,
And that nothing can now stop
The change of consciousness of your humanity.

Rest assured, Children of Earth
That the coming years,
Will be devoted to the construction of bridges.
Bridges between your human part and your divine part.

The tipping point is found to be December 21, 2012.
In fact, your collective consciousness of the past decade
Reinforced by the eminent thought form you have created
Allowed to make a date in the calendar of my fathers
A key date in the history of humankind.

You all have contributed, through your thoughts,
Your wishes, your prayers, meditations and actions,
To create around this date
The exact moment when nothing will be as before.
There will be a before and an after.
December 22, 2012 is now
The date of birth of the new humanity.
Humanity opens to the sixth Sun.

This new cycle is a carrier of life
And much more, it is a resurrection.
The time of inexorable fall is finished.
This is the time of the souls' redemption.
Carried by this wonderful planet that is Earth,
You will learn to respect
And to cherish Earth
Regardless of the piece of land on which you live.

The task ahead is one of construction
You will get rid of the residues,
Outdated habits forgetful of the Sacred
Then rebuild the new world,
A world better than it has ever been.

Children of the Earth, you have entered the period of adolescence
Which gives you access to the divine Manna
and allows you to consider everything,
Your ability to do everything.
It is time to understand you have arrived
At your turn to participate in co-creation.

We the Ancients, Beings from the friendly galaxies,
Star brotherhoods, avatars, guides,
We are, are by your side.

One way or another,
You will soon gradually feel our friendly presence.
You will be able to receive us,
And together we can advance
To assist you in your tentative steps.

I waited for this moment and I am in joy
Because very soon we can be closer.
Do not worry about intrusion, neither invasion
Because it is by no means our intention.
The meeting is adapted to each
According to their degree of openness of consciousness.
Those of you who are most awake
Will host in total.
Those who are more reserved,
Waiting to open to cosmic consciousness,
We will be careful not to rush them into the fire of knowledge.

K'in Batz, the crystal skull of my dear Lacandon friends,
Is the link between you all.
Its presence on the 21 and 22 of December 2012 in Mexico

Brings with it the energy of the old continent
So that you connect between each other.

Just as all the crystal skulls,
The other crystals and hearts in general are now connected
During the passage of December 22,
Feel now the shower of light that
Follows the time that
Announced the birth of a new humanity.

Be happy, dear friends,
Because the emanating link is unbreakable.
It is like the umbilical cord
That gives birth
In the sacred land of your ancestors.

Go in peace, and joy
To the light of the sacred fire burning within you.
Have confidence because you possess
All of everything that you are,
The divine part that is connected to the Universal Source.

I, Pacal Votan, your brother of the light,
I am with you and in your heart.
En Lak'ech, We Are One.
Never forget.
A Lak'en
Pacal Votan. " [5]

---

[5] Pacal Votan Channeling, by Imanna on December 12, 2012 for December 22, 2012. Permission given by Carole Tridon, France via email to publish this message in its entirety with due credit.

Figure 95 - Lol Be December 22, 2012 - to the right of the stele Lorena, Carolina &
Conchita (photo by Carolina)

Chapter 14 – The Portal

December 22, 2012

After that ceremony the crowd mixes and mingles and taking pictures of the stele, the crystal skull, Kin Batz, and the altar. I am beginning to feel unsettled in my stomach. I am concerned that I might be getting the illness Henry got a couple of days ago. I am feeling queasy and would like to go lie down. Some groups have other commitments on their calendar for today like us. Our commitment is to go back to the hotel, pick up the remainder of our group and then head to Chichen Itza. There is discussion among our members about staying here longer or leaving now. The word is passed to meet at the bus in fifteen minutes.

Figure 96 - Lol Be initiation portal 12-22-12

Hunbatz Men has gathered the group in front of the portal that is west of the stele where our ceremony just took place. The portal is a couple of shades of bright orange with seven steps leading up to the portal platform and another six steps heading down once you cross through the portal. He is talking about initiation. He's saying that taking the steps up, going through the portal and then descending the steps on the other side is an initiation. There is a crowd gathered in front of him listening. The musicians are playing again. Our group is scattered. Some of our group is in the crowd about to ascend through the portal while others are gathering to head to the bus.

Carolina gives the word that we will stay a while longer. With that Henry and I too take the seven steps to the top platform. We pass through the portal and descend the six steps on the other side. The number 13 represents the chakras and LOL BE the 13th Flower of Life. We traverse the grass for about twenty yards and join a circle of people surrounding a cross walkway. The Mayan musicians are playing for this group of people from all over the world.

$$\approx \approx \approx$$

Hunbatz invites anyone who would like to share a song to do so. The first to share is Francke Echardour, the crystal skull guardian of Kin Batz. He has an amazing and beautiful voice. He shares a chant. To me the chant sounds like a Native American prayer or song. Everyone feels its power as his voice reverberates into this new day and new cycle. It is so beautiful that when he is complete Hunbatz asks him if he will do it again and the crowd enthusiastically agrees. As Francke's voice again fills the air the crowd is quite pleased, as the song and the delivery are quite extraordinary.

Next Hunbatz invites attendees from different countries of the world to offer a song or chant that will bring the energy from them and their nation to this event. As the songs are being shared I see Brigitte from our group approach Hunbatz and ask if she may have permission to place her crystal skull in the circle. Hunbatz directs her to a spot in the middle and she places it there facing the sun.

The crowd is singing, dancing and clapping as songs are presented by an American, a Mexican, a group of Japanese, a group of Chinese and on it goes. The morning is growing late and I see Carolina circulating through the crowd telling our group that we need to gather at the bus at the end of this song.

The ceremony was wonderful, but I am glad to be heading out. I am not feeling any better as the sun gets higher in the sky this day. I am anxious to get back to the hotel and take something that may help my stomach settle for I do not want to miss the day at Chichen Itza.

Chapter 15 - Hotel Itzamaltun

December 22, 2012

By the time the bus rolls up in front of the Hotel Itzamaltun I know that something is really not in balance for me. I head to the room to drink water and to take some medication to help me settle the queasy stomach. Normally I am not one to take medications, but here I know we are going to be traveling on a bus with out a bathroom and then out in the pyramid park without rest rooms near by. I may not be at my peak, but I do not want to stay at the hotel either. I want to be with the group in Chichen Itza.

At the breakfast table the thought of food is not in the least appealing to me. I have some tea and a bit of bread to help settle my stomach. We grab our hats and day bags and head for the bus to begin the hour and a quarter ride to Chichen Itza.

Chapter 16 – Eh HaY U's Story

December 22, 2012

The bus pulls up along a side street when we reach the area near Chichen Itza. Carolina leaves us to scout out a place for us to have lunch before we enter the park. While she is gone ShavatY shares the story of how Eh Hay U came to her. She talks to us for forty-five minutes. I will do my best to share the highlights as I recall them.

Many of us have been asking ShavatY in the last few days about how she came to be a keeper of a crystal skull. She put us off individually promising to share the story once with the whole group. Now before entering the pyramid park is that time.

Carolina exits the bus on her mission as ShavatY takes the microphone and begins speaking. She has been speaking for only a few minutes when my stomach begins to give me violent signals that its contents are not going to stay put for long.

I lean over to Henry seated to my right and say, "Find me a plastic bag."

He starts asking seatmates near us. Sue, from Australia, sitting in front of Henry, dumps the contents of her plastic shopping bag and passes the bag to Henry in the nick of time. I promptly contribute three deposits into it while seated and the rest of the bus is listening to ShavatY's story.

Henry begins asking others for a second bag, which he gets from Stefan and Bettina in the row behind us. I double bag the liquid and leave it sitting on the pillow in my lap and return my attention to ShavatY. I am enraptured by the story that is unfolding.

ShavatY was still living in Holland when the journey to becoming a keeper of a crystal skull began. She had not sought to find a skull, nor had she any conscious intention of becoming a keeper.

One day during a meditation she had a vision of a male energy that was very bright and benevolent. She didn't connect it with anything in particular, but retained the feeling of that beautiful energy and entity. Not long after, Drunvalo Melchizedek was in Holland for a seminar. During that event there were other gatherings taking place with the people who had come to the seminar. During on of these side gatherings several people were bringing crystal skulls.

The audience was seated and ShavatY was on the isle a few rows back from the front. The skull keepers entered the room from the rear carrying the skulls down the center isle past ShavatY on the way to the front where there was a table awaiting to house the crystal skulls. As the skulls, in the hands of their keepers, began their journey down the aisle ShavatY's body began to shake and gyrate much to the embarrassment of her husband who was sitting beside her. This physical shaking continued as all the crystal skulls entered the room and made their way to the front finally being placed on the table.

After all the skulls were positioned the physical sensations ceased in ShavatY. What she heard or sensed in her inner knowing was that the crystal skulls were very disappointed. They were positioned in on the table in such a manner that their power shut down. They were positioned in a pattern that did not allow for them to connect or communicate. They were very excited to be coming together and were looking forward to having their power put to use and then nothing. The people who had set it all up just didn't understand what was needed. When all the power in the crystal skulls shut down so did the shaking in ShavatY.

After this encounter ShavatY began getting in her meditations indications that she was to become a keeper of a crystal skull. This went on for some time until she felt the knowing that it had to be. She contacted a local gemstone dealer in Holland who traveled many places, including Brazil, purchasing crystals and stones for his shop. She let the dealer know that if he came across a crystal skull in his travels that she could be interested.

Not long after the stone dealer left for Brazil on a shopping trip where he encountered three crystal skulls. He called ShavatY and told her about them. She checked in with her guidance and did not get any energetic connection or feeling with any of them. Not getting an inner hit or feeling on any of them she asked if he could send her pictures. Her thought was that as a visual person if she could see them then maybe she could get a sense or connection. Really, as she came to learn later, this was a test for her.

The dealer without any confirmation from ShavatY came home without any skull. A couple of weeks later he called ShavatY and said that his partner, still in Brazil, had found another crystal skull. Was she interested?

He barely got the words out of his mouth and ShavatY was connected to that same male beautiful, brilliant and benevolent energy she had felt in her vision a while back. She knew instantly that this was the skull for her. She told the dealer, "Yes, I want that skull."

The dealer asked, "You don't want to see a picture first?"

"No," she said, "that's not necessary."

The assistant still in Brazil was walking in the hall in the hotel where the rock and gem show was being held when a man, a stranger, tapped him on the shoulder. The stranger told him while pointing to a door across the hall that in that room over there were two Indians from the mountains and they had a crystal skull in a box under their table. The assistant had never told anyone he was looking for a crystal skull so this was strange, however he decided to see if what the man said was true. He entered the room and easily found the two native gentlemen and asked them if they had a crystal skull.

They lifted the cloth covering their table and showed him that indeed they did in a box underneath. He inquired as to the cost. They gave him the figure. The assistant realized that he did not have that amount of cash this late in his buying trip and verbalized that.

Another man, another stranger, came up to him and said not to worry, "I'll give you the money."

With the skull purchased and in a box, the assistant gem dealer carried it to his car and drove back to his hotel. When he came out of the hotel later his rental car had been stolen. He was a foreigner in a country that didn't speak his native language, but rather than calling the police about his stolen car containing this precious cargo, he inexplicably begins to walk instead. He walks for many blocks when suddenly there in front of him he sees the car abandoned and the doors open. He runs up to it and is relieved to find the crystal skull sitting on the seat in a box.

Meanwhile, back in Holland, it's the day after the dealer has called ShavatY about the crystal skull. She has been thinking about it and realizes she didn't even ask how much the skull would cost. She picked up the phone and called the dealer and he told her.

She hung up the phone contemplating the amount. She and her husband had been living in an older home on the outskirts of town that needed some work. Knowing this they started putting away some money to do updates and repairs to their home. After the phone call to the dealer, ShavatY looked at their house repair savings account to see how much money they had saved. When she looked she found that the balance in the account was the exact amount that the dealer had quoted her to the penny.

The next question was how to communicate this to her husband and have him agree! She thought about it all day. That night her husband, a very powerful clairvoyant, came home and sat her down and looked her in the eye and asked, "Are you sure that you are being called to become a skull keeper?"

"Yes, I'm sure," she told him.

"Do you have any doubts about this being something you must do?," he asked.

She replied, "No, I do not have any doubts."

138

"Okay then," he affirms, "We have to do it."

A few weeks passed and ShavatY was still awaiting the arrival of the skull in Holland. She called the gem dealer to find that the box holding the crystal skull was lost in transit in New York at the airport. The dealer cannot tell her when or even "if" the crystal skull would arrive. ShavatY hung up the phone and went into meditation to connect and see what she could find out. Upon connecting she was told not to worry that the crystal skull would be coming. He, the skull, had some work to do cleaning some things up. His arrival would be delayed a few days.

Sure enough in a few days Eh HaY U finally arrived. ShavatY spent months just sitting with him, building dimensional connections, before she ever learned his name. She's been working with him now for over 17 years.

Chapter 17 – Lunch and Bottle Dancing

December 22, 2012

Carolina returned during ShavatY's story. As the tale concludes she is anxious to get us to the restaurant. Quickly the bus drives off under her direction. I am only vaguely aware of my surroundings. I just know it's hot and there is no ocean breeze like back home, just the relentless Yucatan sun. The bus empties and I stay put just composing myself. I deliver the bag of liquid that's been sitting in my lap the whole time to Henry. He goes inside to get me some paper towels both wet and dry. The bus driver tells me to take my time, but be sure to lock the door when I leave to protect everyone's belongings on the bus.

By the time I join everyone in the restaurant most are already eating their lunch. It is a buffet, which makes serving a large group like ours easy. Henry is sitting at the end of the table with the two gals from California, Miryam and Bonnie. These two ladies live in California and work in different cities for the same company. They've known each other for many years and have traveled together frequently. I join them for good conversation, but consume only water.

As lunch progresses the music starts and the waitresses in native costumes begin dancing. For the second they dance again, but this time they dance while balancing beer bottles on top of their heads. If that wasn't enough at the song's completion, they fill the bottles with water and dance a third time balancing full beer bottles. It's all quite amazing and entertaining. As we file out of the restaurant they pass the donations basket for the entertainment.

Figure 97 - 12-22-12 waitress dancing with beer bottle on her head (photo by Hana)

Chapter 18 - Chichen Itza Ceremony

December 22, 2012

Chichen Itza is probably the most well known pyramid park in the Yucatan. It's evident from the sea of buses as we pull up to the entrance to disembark. The buses, once empty of passengers, must move on to other parking areas to make room for the next wave of buses. There are throngs of people. My last visit here was in 1985. At that time we parked in a dirt parking lot just outside the ball court and walked directly into the park a few feet away. Much has changed since then.

No longer is there a simple parking lot; today we have a whole entrance complex. Outside there are rows of vendor shops and hawkers. The newest gadget being sold everywhere you turn is a wooden noisemaker that emits the sound of a jaguar when you blow into it. It doesn't take long to find this gadget exceptionally irritating.

Today one must wait in a long line just to purchase tickets. Inside the ticket complex is a shop for post cards, books, maps and memorabilia, restaurants, bars, ice cream vendors and rest rooms. We wait for Carolina to purchase the tickets which takes so long our bus driver is volunteering to go around to another side entrance to see if he can speed things up. Alas Carolina gets through and we line up at the turnstiles as she hands us our ticket one by one. After each person passes through we stop and regroup waiting for the rest of the group to enter. Looking around I see we are flanked with vendor tables lining the entrance path as far as the eye can see. The jaguar calls are repeating almost non-stop. Trinkets, necklaces, stone carved pyramids, baskets, hats, jaguar whistles and more adorn vendor tables everywhere you look.

Carolina calls to the group she is one ticket short. Everyone is to check their stub to see if anyone has two ticket stubs stuck together. Sure enough Enid has a double stub. Bianca runs the stub back to the turnstile so her mom, Michaela, can enter and the group can move forward.

≈ ≈ ≈

We meander the path for about a quarter mile before we reach the park. Instead of heading to the main temple, the Castillo, we follow ShavatY who turns right and heads southwest.

We arrive at what ShavatY calls the Queens Temple and the guidebooks call The High Priest's Grave (Osario or Ossuary). It is a four-sided pyramid with a stairway on each side. Similar to the main temple, the Castillo, this smaller pyramid has serpents adorning the sides of the stairs. Coming down the stairs are intertwining symbols like a figure eight that culminate in a serpent head at the ground.

We sit on a short wall across from the thirty-foot high temple. Still feeling queasy I am grateful to be sitting. ShavatY tells us of how the main Castillo is the male energy of this place. That energy, the male energy, has been in charge here for the last cycle, the last 13,000 years. Today is the first day of the new cycle, the female cycle, so we have come here to this pyramid of the female energy.

Figure 98 - Serpent stairs of the Queens Temple Chichen Itza 12-22-12

She has us observe the markings on the pyramid. Notice the pattern coming down the sides of the stairs. The pattern represents our DNA.

We will do a download of energy from this pyramid that will be an upgrade to our DNA. Afterwards we will go around to the backside and do a meditation. From there, when we feel complete, we are make our way individually back to the Castillo in walking meditation and take with us this feminine energy to share with the male pyramid, the main pyramid. This will bring balance to the new energies coming in at this time. We are here today, the first day of this new cycle, to bring the energies of Mother Earth and the female to the male.

Figure 99 - Serpent head (photo by Hana)

Figure 100 - Andean Cross (image from Wikipedia)

At this point, she and Carolina remove their necklaces so that we may use the pendants. She explains that it is an Andean Cross or Chankana. A three-stepped symmetric "cross" with a hole in the center. ShavatY demonstrates that we are each to take the pendant and hold it up to our eye. We are to focus on and through the hole. We are to begin at the top of the pyramid and look through the pendant. We shall draw our attention, focused through the hole in the pendant, down the steps of the pyramid. As our hand with the pendant moves downward, and our gaze and hand descend we will be performing a download of energy into our energetic bodies.

The two pendants make their way around. On my turn I do as instructed. I begin to gaze through the hole in the center of the pendant while focusing at the top f the pyramid. Then I feel the energy change as my hand and gaze descend step by step. Sensations of green and red energy flow over me. It feels more solid the further down I go. When I reach the bottom I pass the pendant to my left. Others are performing their download and we wait for everyone to complete before we head around to the backside.

So as not to draw attention to our group as doing any kind of ceremony we gradually in pairs and small groups meander to the backside. There we spread out and get comfortable and do our own meditations connecting with the western face of this pyramid. Some of the group connects with the sensation of a portal here. Others see many colors, vivid colors of many shades in geometric forms. Others connect with vortexes swirling as they meditate also very colorful.

I find a comfortable spot sitting on a rock and leaning my back against a tree. I feel the coolness the shade of the tree brings. I settle in and let myself relax. I too connect with the pyramid and experience sensations of color, mostly blues and whites with some wisps of pink. I ask to be the deliverer of feminine energy from here to the Castillo. I sense soft waves coming toward me and over me. I don't try to understand intellectually I just feel it.

Soon I feel the gentle touch on my shoulder and I hear Carolina's voice say, "Open your hand."

Figure 101 - Hunab Ku

I open my hand and into it she places a necklace with a black leather cord bearing a gold pendant. The pendant is the symbol of Hunab Ku, the Great Spirit in the center of the galaxy.

She folds my hand closed over the pendant and says, "This is a gift. It is an initiation. When you complete your meditation here walk to the Castillo and share the feminine energies there. After you complete the sharing you may put the necklace on."

I continue with my meditation until I sense that I'm ready to move on. As I leave I study the intricate symbols on north face of this pyramid. I continue in walking meditation back to the main pyramid. I see others from our group making their way. The man made jaguar calls permeate the air from many directions. I wonder what the living animals think of these constant cat calls. Does it upset them or confuse them?

As I approach the main pyramid I walk around the different faces looking for an area where there are fewer tourists. I would like to make my connection without being surrounded by people talking and taking pictures. I find the east face the least crowded. I wait for an opening near the rope cordoning off the pyramid. A group taking a photo exits and leaves a space. I approach.

I hold in my hand a kernel of white corn and my gift, a rose quartz gemstone, to share the energies of our journeys and ceremonies through the Yucatan with Chichen Itza. I kneel in the grass and feel the different energy of this male temple. It feels more solid and heavier than the previous temple. I sit and connect.

When I feel ready I place the corn kernel in the grass and offer this representation of the energies of the new age to this place. Next I put the rose quartz inside the roped off area and offer the energies of our travels and our ceremonies over the last few days to the Castillo. I thank the male energy for holding the ancient knowledge for us during the last 13,000 years so that it is available now to be awakened. I am grateful. Lastly I offer the female energies from the Queen's Temple, that I gathered just moments ago at the smaller temple. I ask that this female energy be accepted and used to balance the energies that are emerging. I offer the message that the female energy has awakened and is sharing its joy.

Feeling a sense of acceptance and completion, I sit back and smile taking in the beauty of this structure. I open my left hand that is still holding the necklace with the golden pendant of Hunab Ku and I release the clasp and encircle my neck to complete the initiation.

≈ ≈ ≈

Henry has been off doing his own process, but now I hear from others in our group that he is looking for me. Believe it or not cell phones work in the jungles of the Yucatan. We connect by phone and coordinate a place to meet.

Figure 102 - symbols at Chichen Itza (photo by Hana)

We spend about a half an hour or more walking around checking out the carvings on the buildings through the binoculars Henry carries. We visit the courtyard of a thousand columns, and other buildings near by. Then suddenly I know I have to find a ladies room and quickly. We make our way to the side of the Castillo where the public restrooms are located.

Figure 103 - symbols at Chichen Itza (photo by Hana)

Figure 104 - symbols at Chichen Itza (photo by Hana)

Figure 105 – Chac Mool Chichen Itza (photo by Hana)

Figure 106 – Courtyard of a 1000 columns Chichen Itza (photo by Hana)

Figure 107 - Jaguar at Chichen Itza (photo by Hana)

Figure 108 - symbols at Chichen Itza

From my last visit almost thirty years ago I have a distinct memory of the sacred cenote. Just days ago we made a dive inside a cenote. I have a strong desire to visit the cenote here at Chichen Itza today, but due to my upset stomach it feels like the right time to head back to the entrance instead.

≈ ≈ ≈

Back at the entrance complex we visit the store to purchase some Imodium so I can make the bus ride back to Izamal. The clerk pulls out a box and asks me how many I want.

When I tell her I'll take the box she says it will be $18.00 US. Wow!

How much for one pill?

That is $2.00 for a single pill. I take two pills knowing that the price is exorbitant, but I have no choice.

With the park due to close soon there are no lines at the ticket purchase booth and the entrance area is virtually empty. Henry and I sit in the atrium and one by one our group starts gathering. Carolina arrives with a cup full of ice cream. She starts a trend and soon almost everyone visits the ice cream shop except me. The ice cream looks good and I am hungry, but dairy on this stomach doesn't sound like a smart thing consume when I face a long bus ride back to Izamal.

In just a few minutes the first of our group will be breaking off and heading in other directions instead of boarding the bus back to Izamal. Myrtha is heading to Ecuador. Miryam and Bonnie are heading to Cancun to stay overnight and catch their flight back to California in the morning. The bus driver opens the under compartment of the bus and pulls out their luggage as everyone is snapping photos, swapping contacts, hugging and exchanging final sharings. The taxi is patiently waiting to take the three ladies to Cancun. Eventually the last of the good-byes said, they depart and the rest of us file onto our bus and return for our last night in Izamal.

Chapter 19 – Coba and Tulum

December 23, 2012

I wake fully rested at 7:00am in our now familiar homestead the sound of the jungle serenades me through the shuttered windows. Our bags are packed except for our toiletry items needed this morning. Today is our last day on the bus. Tonight, at the end of our day's travels, our group settles into the hotel, Las Golondrinas, in Playa del Carmen.

Our numbers are dwindling more and more. ShavatY has returned to Playa del Carmen and shall meet up with us again in a few days. This morning after breakfast Mindy and Sue will catch a cab to the Cancun airport. Ines leaves us at Coba later today and a couple more, Renate and Enid, are to depart after a couple of days in Playa.

Hugs, photos and good byes are shared in the lobby full luggage. Our faithful and adaptable driver is there read to fill the belly of the bus with our bags that now overflow onto the sidewalk. Not long after our final wave to the cab we fill the bus and depart ourselves.

The official tour ended with yesterday's ceremony at Chichen Itza. Today begins the extended portion of the trip through December 27th. Carolina has employed a guide, Israel, for today's journey to Coba and Tulum. His voice is weak and hoarse, as he has just completed a week as one of the speakers with Greg Braden's tour through the Yucatan.

≈ ≈ ≈

Our home on wheels the last few days pulls away from the curb and through town for one last time as the sun spills through the leaves and we bounce over the speed bumps as we exit. After a few hours ride southeast the bus pulls into a colorful and bustling parking lot just outside the park entrance. As to be expected, there are vendor stands and restaurants surrounding the parking area.

As Carolina heads off to purchase our entrance vouchers we mill around the shops. Henry, standing in front of a display of Mayan calendar replicas, picks one up and studies the center figure which is a face with the tongue sticking out. He mimics the expression by sticking out his own tongue and muses out loud, " I wonder what it means?"

Two of our companions nearby begin to explain that it has a very specific meaning. It is there to educate and remind the people that sticking the tongue out to catch the sun's rays is very important for maintaining a healthy body. That makes sense to me. The sun is where we get out vitamin D and the tongue and the saliva are where we quite easily, readily and quickly absorb nutrients directly into our system. That is really fascinating.

I think how much clarity this simple piece of information has brought. There is so much significance and meaning that has been conveyed to us through symbols that we are ignorant of. How much more out there is not just pretty pictures and symbols, but rather messages to be interpreted? What other wisdom and knowledge from centuries past has been preserved and communicated yet not understood?

It's so obvious that these cultures that built the Mayan empire were advanced. Their cities are vast, hundreds of acres, with only tiny sections that have been uncovered and even smaller sections that have been restored. How much of what they were trying to tell us have we actually received? How much of our interpretations of their information is correct and how much is inaccurate? Were we meant to find these archeological and historic sites? Were we meant to find them now in the last fifty to a hundred years before the dawn of this new age? Is there a message or maybe many messages for us here?

One pyramid city holds so much I could spend a month here and still not comprehend the full significance. Also there are layers within layers: the societal layer, the cultural, the astronomical, the spiritual, the scientific, the leadership and other layers each with their own information and viewpoint.

$$\approx \approx \approx$$

We enter Coba and proceed to the ball court area. Israel is telling us of the Mayan culture and the different theories and reasons their culture became extinct. He tells us that Mayaland existed in the areas that we know today as the Mexican states of Jalisco, Chiapas, Yucatan and Campeche as well as in the countries of Belize, Guatemala and Honduras. In the height of the culture there were over 4,000 major Mayan cities and over 12,000 Mayan sites.

Figure 109 - Coba 12-23-12

He says that many things played a part in the collapse such as wars, drought, infighting for power, abuse of the working class, and most importantly the over exploitation of mother nature. Like today, he says, they lived in the gratification of the now without thinking of future consequences. Take trees for example. They learned to make plaster for stucco by combining burned limestone ashes with water and the resin from the rubber tree. Stucco erodes and needs care. In order to maintain their cities, they cut down the trees to the point that erosion and flooding became monumental problems leading to environmental disasters.

The 52-year cycles were very important to the Mayans. Israel tells us how on the last night of a cycle there was celebration and then the next day they would begin building a new temple on top of the old one. This is why today there are many layers to most of the pyramids in Mayaland.

The leaders, and only the leaders, lived in the city proper. They lived on top of the pyramids and servers brought their food, water and whatever they needed. The working class lived outside the cities farming and raising animals. They were only allowed into the cities for rituals.

Another interesting thing that Israel shares with our group is that NASA (National Aeronautics and Space Administration of the USA) uses the Mayan calendar for its exacting accuracy. I had already heard that from Drunvalo. It is interesting to hear it also from this Mayan scholar.

Figure 110 - Coba December 23, 2012

Figure 111 - Coba main pyramid (Henry & Jadranka

We eventually make our way to the main pyramid. Our group huddles a few yards from the stairs and Carolina leads us in a short meditation to feel the energies of this place. In return we share the energies we've gathered in our travels from the ceremonies and the awakening with this site. Spreading and connecting that is part of the mission and the journey.

Many in the group climb to the top to feel the powerful energy in that space. Henry and I, both still feeling a little off balance from being ill, climb part way up and sit with Carolina visiting and looking out over the city.

≈ ≈ ≈

In order to conserve time, we hire bicycle taxis for the return rather than walking. Two and three at a time we are deposited at the entrance. When our group is complete, we board the bus for a short ride to the restaurant which over looks the lake outside the pyramid city of Coba. It is quite unusual to see an above ground lake in the Yucatan. There are hundreds of miles of underwater rivers and caverns, but almost no above ground lakes.

As our diminishing group of 18 settles in for lunch at one long outdoor table, I look up to see Sophia at the lake's edge. There is a platform or deck overlooking the lake where she stands, back to us, facing the lake. Her long blonde hair flowing in the slight breeze and a white shawl settles over her shoulders. I can tell by the movement of her arms she is cleaning energy again.

When I ask her about this later, she tells me it just started coming to her in the last few months. She can feel and sense the darkness and denseness of the energy around her and has a compelling desire to clean and clear it. When the task is complete she senses that as well. I admire her for following her inner guidance and doing what she is called to do.

≈ ≈ ≈

Our arrival in Tulum is later than expected. After disembarking the bus and taking bathroom breaks, we rush to catch a tram. A tram? This is so different from my last visit in March of 1985. In that year the park entrance was located at the tram drop off. The ticket booth area of today was then a dirt floor restaurant. Today the old entrance is blocked off and the new entrance winds you around a jungle trail for a half-mile before get into the pyramid city. One thing I will say is, "take good walking shoes!"

When we finally enter the park Israel, our guide, hurriedly points out a couple of interesting architectural designs and symbols, like the face in the corner of one building.

Figure 112 - Tulum December 23, 2012

Then we head to the top of the hill to get the view of the sea from behind the temple. This is the only pyramid site in Mexico with a breathtaking view of the ocean within it walls. After snapping a few photos, the guards begin calling for everyone to exit the park, as it is closing time.

Figure 113 - Tulum face in the building

Figure 114 - Tulum looking out to sea

Figure 115 - Tulum - Henry & Kathryn

Upon exiting the park I see that Sophia and Brigitte are still outside the ticket booth area in the grass with another lady, a stranger not a part of our group. It is obvious they are intent on doing some kind of energy work and cleaning. The last group of trams pulls up and the departing visitors quickly and easily fill up the first two trams. We move on to the third. Seats are a premium and I get invited to sit on Jadranka's lap for the ride back. Just as the bus jerks into motion to leave here come Sophia and Brigitte running to jump on in the nick of time. They tell how they were cleaning again and felt compelled to stay and complete their work, even if it had meant walking back to the bus.

≈ ≈ ≈

The sun sets quickly in the tropics and in a very short time of rolling down the highway, the sky darkens, as our home on wheels carries us north to Playa del Carmen. About 8:30 in the evening we roll up in front of the hotel with a surprise in store for our driver.

He has been extremely accommodating and cordial, so much so he feels like a member of the group. Everyone circles the fountain in front of the hotel holding hands as Carolina re-boards the bus to invite our driver to join us. Stepping inside our circle, Carolina presents the driver with an envelope bulging with cash to express our appreciation. She sings his praises and thanks him for his exemplary service. After Merry Christmas greetings and hugs all around he departs for home and an evening with his own family.

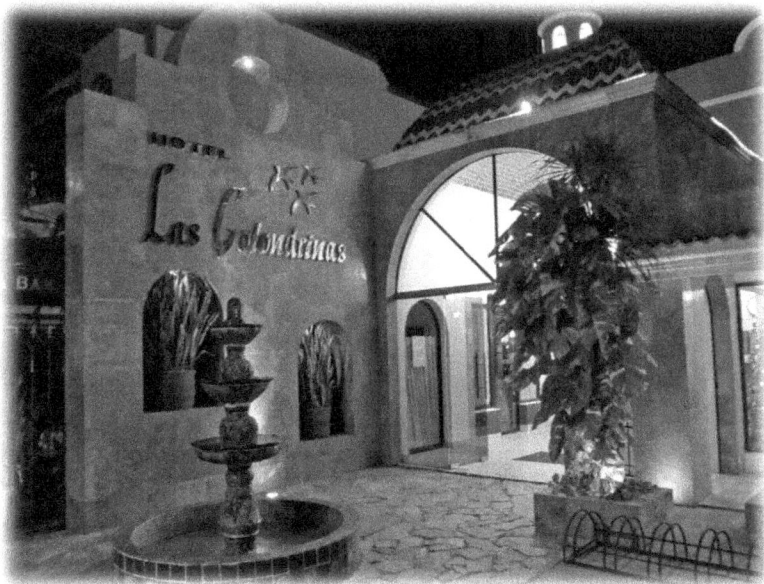

Figure 116 - Las Golondrinas Hotel entrance (photo by Brigitte)

Figure 117 - December 2012 transformation (photo by Brigitte)

Over the next few days the paths of our group crisscross in town, at the hotel, and on the beach as we shop, dive, sun bath, play and take day trips. One in our group, Beate, even goes for a haircut, an outward symbol of her inward transformation, during her travels of the last three weeks. Carolina posts notices daily in the lobby for our group activities. We gather for dinner on a couple of occasions where Bianca performs brilliantly as our banker tallying up the checks.

Figure 118 - Christmas Eve gifts - Carolina, Jadranka & Henry

Christmas Eve Carolina reserves the upstairs room of a restaurant on Fifth Avenue and our group gathers to celebrate. Henry wraps up a copy of his novel, Secotan, and gifts everyone at dinner. That night and throughout the next day the hotel lobby (the only place to get cell service in the hotel) is filled with snippets of conversations and laughter shared with families far away for the Christmas holidays.

Figure 119 - Internet connection and socializing in the lobby, Sophia and Erik (photo by Brigitte)

The intense and chaotic party energy of Fifth Avenue is such a contrast to what we've experienced over the last few days it is difficult to spend too much time there. The three "play days" fly by quickly. The notice board is no longer displaying future events but rather departure times on the 28th so we can gather in the lobby to send each other off. Quickly the last full day in Playa del Carmen dawns and we are ready to end our gathering with a ceremony.

Figure 120 - Christmas Day 2012

Figure 121 - Kathryn & Henry moonlight meditation 12-26-12

Figure 122 - Sophia & Brigitte

Figure 123 - moonlight meditation 12-26-12

Chapter 20 – Sunrise Ceremony on the Beach

December 27, 2012

Today is our last day in the Yucatan. We meet in the lobby of Hotel Las Golondrinas at 6:30am, the rag tag remnants of the group that gathered nine days ago. Christmas has come and gone. We've played tourist for a few days. Half of the travelers have returned home or continued their travels elsewhere. The dozen or so who remain gather to hear ShavatY tell us that there is a very powerful vortex of unmanifest creative energy in Playa del Carmen which draws a lot of creative people to the area: writers, poets, artists, etc. There is also a shadow side vortex that is demonstrated by the Fifth Avenue, party life and chaotic energy of Playa del Carmen.

In a few minutes, we will walk to the beach, hang a left and walk along the sand to the last undeveloped parcel of ocean front land located at 24th Street. Several have tried to develop this land, but the development has never moved forward. Each time there is a reason why: the deal falls apart, the money doesn't come or the project doesn't get approved. Something happens that results in this last surviving connection between Mother Ocean and the Mother Earth remaining open. This parcel, expansive enough for a large hotel and gardens, is surrounded by a cement block wall and watched over by private security guards. The ocean side of this wall has become a canvas for local artists. A wonderful, colorful, and varied mural decorates this small oasis surrounded by hotels of steel and glass.

Walking from the hotel to our destination on the beach, we each pick brightly colored flowers and blossoms to adorn the ceremonial altar. Upon arrival ShavatY begins by laying out the festive altar cloth. Next she spills a bagful of flower petals from a local florist onto the altar. Then she pulls banana, orange, kiwi, and other fruits from her bag. Of-course, Eh HaY U anchors the altar and crystals, skulls, wands and other items belonging to group members are arranged around him.

We start our meditation by connecting with the energies of our journeys, not just the current journeys to Peru, Bolivia and the Yucatan, but also our personal journeys that brought us to this place. Playa del Carmen is a test for all who connect here. We are here to feel this new energy and practice staying connected in our hearts, even with all the distractions and chaos on Fifth Avenue. A test that helps prepare us for taking this new energy back into our world, the world where we return to our daily lives. Once there we are to share it through our living example. We sink into the feelings and connect with all the dimensions, beings, etheric energies, fairies, elementals, beings that have crossed over, guardians, angels, etc. We connect with Mother Ocean.

ShavatY comes around and once again connects each of us with Eh HaY U. It is our final ceremony with this handsome and magnificent clear crystal skull, at least for this journey. Once complete with the meditation we walk into the surf connecting with Mother Ocean. We offer gifts of flowers from the altar with the intent of sending the new energies out into the world through this pervasive body of water that colors this planet blue. Thank you, Mother.

Returning to the altar, ShavatY enlists the men to come forward. She invites them to take on the role of the new male energy for the next 13,000 years, the nurturer. The three men, Henry, Erik and Stefan, cut up the fruit and traverse the circle, serving each of the women as they go. The sun's rays shine through as the men begin serving and nurturing the women, as if Father Sky is approving. The women accept the role of receiving fully, in this way they are gifting back to the men.

Figure 124 - Sunrise ceremony Stefan, Erik and Henry (photo by Carolina)

ShavatY proffers for one last time the invitation to take one kernel of the ancient red corn and some of the white corn imbued with the new energies. This time it is for us to take home with us to our part of the world. This invitation is for any who feels called to do ceremony on March 21, 2013. She tells us that the energies awakened on December 12, 2012 and December 21, 2012 will be balancing out and aligning. Every day now these energies, that have been birthed in the darkness of the winter in these short days with the sun closest to earth, will be stretching, awakening and coming fully into alignment for the Spring Equinox the balancing point.

The ceremony continues with an offering to Mother Earth. One by one we take a large, green, tropical leaf from the altar and garnish it with some of the flowers and fruits from the altar. Placing these leaflet offerings on the colorfully painted wall behind us, we make our silent prayers of thanks to Mother Earth. All the remaining items on the altar are then gifted to the birds, squirrels, iguanas and local animals by placing them along the wall.

The private guard and care taker of this land, a local dark skinned Mexican man inside the wall, at first starts removing our offerings. He sees that more and more are coming and that he is not intimidating us. Finally he gives up and just watches as the wall is adorned in fruit and fauna.

Figure 125 - At the Cafe after Ceremony (photo by Hana)

Chapter 21 - Eh Hay U

December 27, 2012

Henry and I take advantage of the opportunity to have a private session with Eh HaY U. Henry is scheduled for noon so I head to town. My goal is to find a few souvenirs and items for my altar back home. On Calle Corazon, a tree lined pedestrian street off of Fifth Avenue near 10th, I find a shop with authentic native artisan crafts from around Mexico, not machine made items. I leave with a couple of treasures in my bag that include an altar cloth and red wooden box with a heart on top for my corn. Knowing only that I want a couple of souvenirs, I meander in and out of shops on 5th Ave. I am attracted to some heart shaped metal ornaments. I don't know their intended purpose, but what came to me was hanging them on the wall over the door signifying that all who enter this home enter in love. Perfect. That's the extent of my souvenir shopping.

I keep wandering looking for a skull for my altar to represent the energy of Eh HaY U. Not a crystal skull, just something as a representation. Not sure what I want. I find many painted paper mache skulls. They don't appeal to me. Finally in a shop I come upon a small black ceramic skull. It feels good to me. I pick it up at the same time that my phone rings. It's Henry.

ShavatY has had to postpone. Something has come up and she needs to Skype her family in Holland. We have time for lunch before Henry's appointment. Back to the hotel, Henry and I go off to "Natural Market" restaurant on 30th Avenue. It's a wonderful local restaurant with an awesome organic menu. We have gigantic smoothies and share a salad for lunch.

≈ ≈ ≈

ShavatY is sitting in the atrium of the hotel, with her pink backpack, when we return from lunch. Henry, ShavatY, and Eh HaY U go to our room 102 for his session. Sitting in the atrium I realize I can't use our room to go to the bathroom and there is not one in the hotel lobby. Well I have to pick up our dive gear and I know there's a bathroom there, so off I go. My intention is to take a taxi back, but I'm really in no rush. After picking up our gear and settling our tab at the dive shop, I slowly roll the bulky black dive bag full of gear from 4th Street to 20th street. Some curbs without ramps and a few bumps here and there make things interesting. In less than an hour roundtrip, I park the bag outside our room and relax in a lounge chair beside the pool in the open-air atrium.

Figure 126 - Atrium in Las Golondrinas (photo by Brigitte)

Figure 127 - Pool Las Golondrinas (photo by Brigitte)

I must have dozed, because soon I hear Henry commenting on the dive bag. I wake and join them. He doesn't believe that I walked the dive gear back. He shares briefly some of his amazing experience. He's excited to record what he remembers and grabs his notebook and pen before settling in at the wrought iron table in the atrium outside our room.

I join ShavatY in our room. She explains sequentially how the session will take place. Eh HaY U will open many dimensions and connect me with them. He will open and connect to the place I came from. Not Earth as none of us originally came from Earth, as it is too young. We all came from someplace in the stars originally a long, long time ago. Eh HaY U will connect with that place. When ShavatY senses the connection she will chant in whatever language comes through from that place or dimension. She tells me that I may get images, places or memories coming to me. Then at that point I will be able to ask questions with my inner voice of Eh HaY U. He will line me up dimensionally with the answer. The answers may click immediately or the answers may integrate sometime over the next six months.

I lay down on the bed diagonally with my head in the upper left corner and my feet in the lower right corner. Placed on the bed at my head facing my crown chakra is Eh HaY U. At my feet is ShavatY holding space. A few minutes go by and I feel as if someone is walking in the room. My mind jumps to the thought that Henry has come into the room to use the bathroom. But that is not true. Henry is not in the room. Then I feel a presence standing behind ShavatY a strong, tall, well-built, amber skinned male. He doesn't say anything. However he stays and stands over ShavatY watching over me and the process. I can feel him looking at me. There is no fear involved, but rather a very protective feeling comes over me.

ShavatY makes the dimensional connection with my place of origin and begins the chant. The words sound beautiful. Consciously I do not know what they mean. My sense is that I know this language, this message. It feels like trying to recall a name or place a song that you are very familiar with. Like the name is on the tip of your tongue. ShavatY's chant is like a short song or story.

At some point I realized that my body feels heavy and that I'm not sure if I can move it. Then I hear ShavatY tell me it is time for me to ask my inner questions. They, the questions, just come flowing from me. I can't remember exactly what I asked, but I remember asking and asking and asking. I did not feel that I got any instant clicks; I am still integrating those dimensional answers. [Like dreaming, if you don't write things down right away you lose them. I know I asked many questions, but I can't remember them. I will have to trust that the answers will come and the ones I need to understand consciously will come in a way that I will remember the asking.]

The session is ending and ShavatY has moved from my feet to my head. She is telling me to come back very, very slowly, especially when opening my eyes. Make that the last thing she says. Opening them too soon before you are energetically fully returned to this dimension can cause headaches. I try to move my fingers, just a bit, like I do coming out of meditation. I can't move them. Not at first and not for a while. I am amazed that I was so deep that motor function doesn't return immediately. It takes a while and I eventually am able to move my body parts and open my eyes. ShavatY explains that doing dimensional work like this we may think we're here in this dimension because our mind has thoughts. However, we come out to the mind level and then go back dimensionally many, many times during a session.

When we return to the wrought iron table in the atrium Carolina is there with Henry and everyone is talking and sharing. I'm in a fog. I am not fully back in this dimension. It is very difficult for me to focus and converse. Looking back it would have been better for me to rest and integrate before joining the real world again.

Chapter 22 - Spring Equinox Ceremony

Three months have passed and today is the day for ceremony. The time has come when the new energies that reached us from the center of our galaxy on December 21, 2012 have balanced out. These energies arrived on the winter solstice, the shortest and darkest day of the year. Months have passed, during which time, the energies have been balancing and stabilizing. Here today, March 21, 2013, the Spring Equinox, their emergence is now more balanced and we celebrate.

I have been planning my ceremony for this day since leaving the Yucatan in December and promising to return the kernel of ancient red corn to Mother Earth on this day. I've invited friends from my Third Thursday Group to join me on the beach tonight for the ceremony.

To represent the birthing of the new energies of spring, I hard-boil some eggs. I then dip each in coloring solution to reflect the bright colors of spring coming forth. So far the number of responses tally to six people attending ceremony, but for some reason I keep hearing in my inner voice that I need to make seven eggs. I, of-course, follow my inner guidance without being sure why. Maybe I am being guided to make the extra one for Diana, my friend who wanted to attend, but is out of town visiting her family.

After boiling and coloring the seven eggs, I paint on each one. On some I draw symbols and images and on all I paint the name of a goddess. Whatever I feel I draw and paint like a star tetrahedron, and eye, circles within circles. I'm having fun. Somehow I get the feeling that the egg meant for me is the raspberry red one bearing the name of the fiery Goddess Pele, the Goddess of the volcano in Hawaii. However, I will let everyone else choose and I will take the last egg, the one not chosen by the others. One by one I place the eggs in a large basket on a bed of crinkle paper names facing down; Pele, Isis, Kuan Yin, Gaia, Hathor, Selene and Brigit.

At the local garden center, I purchase some Snap Dragons that will decorate the altar and then to be gifted to each participant after the ceremony. Again I start to buy a six-pack, but I get the feeling that I need to have seven. Even though the flowers come six-packs and I still have only six responses, I buy two packs so that I can take seven flowers with me. These colorful spring flowers will adorn the altar and symbolize the coming growth this spring and this year.

Remembering the beauty of the many flower petals on our altar in Playa del Carmen three months ago, I wish to find some blossoms or flowers to adorn the altar. It is still early for the blooms in Mother Nature, given our chilly spring. So I stop at a local flower shop and ask if they have petals from flowers that they have pruned back?

"No," she said, "we have all new flowers right now and I don't have any petals today."

"Thank you. I understand," comes my reply as I turned to go. I stop short as a small Shiatsu dog appears out of nowhere silently and I am about to step on him. I apologize and bend down to greet the little fellow and leave.

Turning the key in my ignition, I look up to see the shop owner coming out of the shop towards my car with a bouquet of yellow daisies in her hand. She approaches my driver's door and I roll down my window.

She says, "Here take these. I'm going to throw them away today."

I tell her, "I'm happy to pay you for them."

"No," she says, "they were going to go into the trash. You can have them instead."

"Thank you so much. That is kind."

How cool is that? Thanks universe for the gift. At home I ask for permission to remove their petals and use them in the ceremony.

Astronomically, the spring equinox marks the moment at which the Earth's axis tilts neither away from nor toward the sun and as a result we experience nearly equal periods of daylight and darkness across the globe. Many think of the Spring Equinox as the transit point when the Earth-Sun (Mother-Father) relationship stands in perfect balance. It is equilibrium, yet anticipation.

It represents a time of birth, new growth and expansion, a time when we break the bonds of winter and experience new beginnings. It is a time to take stock of unsettled feelings that may have been hibernating all winter, a time to make apologies or settle them to get into balance.

≈ ≈ ≈

With this state of mind I arrive on the beach and connect to the energy of Mother Earth as I prepare the altar. As my feet hit the sand, I put down my basket and bag. Looking up I see Debbie on the beach already. She is with someone, someone unfamiliar to me. Here is my confirmation on my guidance of number seven. Debbie has met a new friend, Carissa, and she invited her to join our ceremony. How perfect. We are now complete at seven.

Figure 128 - Orbs with Carissa and Debbie

For the altar cloth I choose the hand woven table cloth from Spain that belong to my Abuela (grandmother). I place that on the sand and in the center of that I place the smaller green altar cloth I purchased in Playa del Carmen. Next I place my ceramic skull representing the energy of Eh HaY U in the center. Around that I place some of my crystals, the basket of eggs and the bright yellow Daisy petals. Radiating out in a circle are the seven small Snapdragons. Crystals and sacred objects of the others join the altar as well.

Next comes the lighting of the sweet grass to smudge and cleanse everyone. Delia brought some copal incense from her trip to Palenque on December 21st 2012. That goes into the brass burner to further cleanse, bring balance, and connection between the energies of December 21 and March 21. Circling the altar with our feet in the sands of Mother Earth on this cool spring evening we begin our ceremony.

After lighting the candles we begin by honoring the four directions and inviting in the energies of each direction, East, South, West and

North to be present with us this night. We invite the energy of Mother Earth and Father Sky to join us. We connect with our own inner energy and spirit. We invite the energy of Great Spirit to be with us in the sacred space of this circle.

Figure 129 - 03-21-13 Spring Equinox Ceremony

I tell the story of how I have come to do this ceremony this night in Emerald Isle. Of how I had made an agreement, on December 21st on that patio of the Hotel Itzamaltun in Mexico, to share the energies of the ancient corn with my area on this day of balancing. In my wooden box with the heart on it I have the one kernel of ancient corn. In that same box I brought with me the white corn representing the new energies that are coming. I tell them, "Each of you will take a kernel of white corn after the ceremony and walk the beach to find the place for you to gift your kernel and it's energies back to Mother Earth.

Debbie brought her a crystal bowl that resonates with the heart chakra frequency. We each take turns playing the bowl and make a personal statement about this time of balance. Delia dedicates her bowl song to her dear friend who crossed over today, Joseph Clyde Francis Sullivan III, a master native flute player. Joseph would have loved this ceremony, she tells us.

Figure 130 – Orbs

Figure 131 - Orbs

These are not exactly the exact words of the ceremony, but rather a representation. We speak of Earth's axis and today's equal periods of night and day. We speak of the growth and expansion of spring in general and in reference to new age that is emerging. We take some time to go inside. We reflect on who am I becoming? What am I awakening within myself? What wisdom am I bringing with me from the dark of winter? Now is the time of balance, a time when the veil between the seen and the unseen is thin. Pay attention and see, feel or sense what message or images are coming through.

Now is a time of emergence of energy and expansion; a time where we feel the drive to implement our visions that came during our time of winter rest and dreaming. Now is a time to cleanse, clean, and make room for the growth coming our way. It is a time to clean our altars, our homes, and even our minds.

In springtime the buds come out to stretch into the newly awakening spring. They are vulnerable, yet their strength too is to be honored. Each of you is invited to take home with you a flower from the altar. Plant this flower to represent the growth of your inner and outer dreams.

The egg has long represented new life and birth. After completing the ceremony we will pass the basket and each of us will choose an egg. On the downward face of the egg is the name of a goddess. This represents a goddess with whom you will birth a relationship over this next year.

Take these gifts home and have your own ceremony, dig a hole, place in it your egg, and then your flower and let the new energies awaken in your life.

Figure 132 - Kay, Georgia, Ahna, Delia, Debbie, Carissa 03-21-13

Go within now and connect with Mother Earth and thank her for this time of growth, birth, new energies and balance. Connect with your higher self, angels, guides or whoever shows up for you. When you feel complete take a kernel of white corn then walk and connect until you find a space to gift this corn back to Mother Earth.

Figure 133 - Kay, Georgia, Ahna, Delia, Kathryn & Carissa 03-21-13

I begin breathing and go inside where I make my inner connection. After some minutes I feel complete. I remove the single red kernel of the ancient corn from the wooden box. Kernel in hand I let myself be drawn to the waters edge feeling the waves splash over my toes. Bending down I gently release the sacred morsel into the waters of Mother Ocean with my prayer to spread the ancient energies along with balance, growth and awakening to everyone and everything these waters touch.

Thank you, Mother Earth. We are listening for your guidance during this time of awakening.

Remember now.

[P.S. At the end the basket is passed around and each one selects the egg and Goddess that is perfect for them. There is much excitement and amazement at the perfect synchronicity of the pairings. Carissa, who selects the egg with the star tetrahedron, comments on having seen the shape during this meditation. And, by the way, I did end up with Pele, the fiery one.]

Epilogue

Thank you for coming along on this travel adventure.

As I write this final section I am sitting in the lobby of the Hotel Real de Chapala in Ajijic Mexico on Saturday April 27th, 2013. I am enjoying my day off in the two-week teacher training with Drunvalo Melchizedek's School of Remembering for Awakening the Illuminated Heart. I am feeling the shifting of these new energies coming to life more palpably these days. We are coming into the age where it is becoming more important by the day that we awaken, that we remember and find the way into our hearts. It is time to find that sacred space of creation that is connected to unity consciousness; find that place that feels like home. It is time to remember. It is my wish that this message may in some way help you on your journey.

In La'Kesh and Namaste

$$\approx \approx \approx$$

During teacher training I shared some of the experiences and ceremony stories with my fellow classmates. One evening I was sharing with Corina and Jens. When I finished the story of the reunification of the Condor and Eagle on December 21st, Jens thanked me for doing this reunification work for everyone. This expression of thanks took me by surprise. I hadn't thought of it from that perspective, the perspective of completing a mission of service to others and humanity. I felt humbled and grateful to be allowed to participate. This was very interesting and honoring to see it from this new perspective. Thank you Jens for giving me that gift.

I offer this analogy here to help you understand the pace of unfoldment of the incoming energies. If this coming 13,000 year cycle were the equivalent of one day, then each month that passes would be the equivalent of a half a second. Each year that passes for us would only be 6 seconds in the new cycle. At that pace it would be the equivalent of 9 years of our time for one minute to pass in the new cycle. Be patient and alert the changes are unfolding with time. We can only handle the changes a little at a time so Mother Earth is delivering them in doses that are palatable.

This book talks about fulfilling destiny for those who traveled to the Yucatan in December 2012. That fulfillment has ignited energies that are available now to everyone. With the shift and new energies coming in at this time, each of you reading this book is also being called to opportunities that invite you to fulfill your own destiny.

Awake, remember and fulfill your destiny.

≈ ≈ ≈

Reading List:
Braden, Gregg: Matrix; Power of Prayer; Deep Truth
Braden, Russell, Pinchbeck, Macy, Jenkins and more: The Mystery of 2012
Hand Clow, Barbara: The Mayan Code
Melchizedek, Drunvalo: The Ancient Secrets of the Flower of Life Volume I and Volume II
Melchizedek, Drunvalo: Living in the Heart
Melchizedek, Drunvalo: Mayan Ouroboros
Melchizedek, Drunvalo: Serpent of Light
Sitchin, Zecharia: Genesis Revisited
Talbot, Michael: Holographic Universe
Wilcock, David: The Source Field Investigations

Internet Sites:
- Gregg Braden - **http://www.greggbraden.com/**
- Gaiam TV - **http://www.gaiamtv.com/**
- Kathryn Gorham – **http://www.onetinyspace.com**
- Nassim Haramein - **http://resonance.is/**
- Carolina Hehenkamp Sacred Travel - **http://www.onenesstravel.pranalight.de/**
- Lilou Mace YouTube - **http://www.youtube.com/user/liloumace**
- Drunvalo Melchizedek - **http://drunvalo.net/**
- School of Remembering – **http://theschoolofremembering.com**
- Spirit of Maat - **http://spiritofmaat.com/**
- Spirit Science – YouTube Chanel – original series of 26 videos "Spirit Science" - **http://www.youtube.com/playlist?list=PL2C2FBAB7E002EE3E**
- 2012 – youtube.com "2012 a to z"

About the Author

Kathryn lives on the North Carolina coastal island of Emerald Isle with her husband, Henry, and her rescue dog, Maya. She appreciates the wonderful views offered by Mother Nature from her home overlooking the sound.

She enjoys beach walks, which is the perfect outlet for the stress of daily routines. Not being a morning person she enjoys more sunsets than sunrises.

She is passionate about the subject of changing times and has been on her path of growth and awakening since 1980. She is also a certified teacher of the School of Remembering® and currently teaches Awakening the Illuminated Heart® workshops. Kathryn is also a practicing REALTOR®. She holds a Broker license and she lists and sells homes along the beautiful Crystal Coast of North Carolina.

Visit Kathryn's website at:
http://www.OneTinySpace.com/fulfillingdestiny
OneTinySpace@gmail.com

[Front cover photo taken by Kathryn at Mayapan on the morning of December 21, 2012.]

www.ingramcontent.com/pod-product-compliance
Lightning Source LLC
Chambersburg PA
CBHW060923040426
42445CB00011B/768